Managing for Performance

Managing
for
Performance

Delivering Results

Through Others

Pam Jones

PEARSON
Prentice Hall
BUSINESS

Harlow, England • London • New York • Boston • San Francisco • Toronto
Sydney • Tokyo • Singapore • Hong Kong • Seoul • Taipei • New Delhi
Cape Town • Madrid • Mexico City • Amsterdam • Munich • Paris • Milan

PEARSON EDUCATION LIMITED

Edinburgh Gate
Harlow CM20 2JE
Tel: +44 (0) 1279 623623
Fax: +44 (0) 1279 431059
Website: www.pearsoned.co.uk

First published in Great Britain in 2007

ISBN: 978-0-273-70354-9

British Library Cataloguing-in-Publication Data
Jones, Pam, 1960-
    Managing for performance : delivering results through others / Pam Jones.
    p. cm.
    Includes bibliographical references and index.
    ISBN 978-0-273-70354-9
    1. Management.   2. Leadership.   I. Title.

HD31.J625 2007
658.4'092--dc22

                                                                    2007060096

Library of Congress Cataloging-in-Publication Data
A catalog record for this book is available from the Library of Congress

10 9 8 7 6 5 4 3 2 1
10 09 08 07

Typeset in 11.5 pt Minion by 3
Printed by Ashford Colour Press Ltd., Gosport

The publisher's policy is to use paper manufactured from sustainable forests.

The publisher is grateful to Sage Publications for permission to reproduce the self-assessment questionnaire 'Identifying your assumptions' on pp 4–6.

Contents

Introduction

Every manager is judged on performance. Yours and that of your team. Continually improving your team's performance is an essential part of your role, but it's not always easy. You need to deal with individual issues – from persistent poor performance to high performers who have lost their motivation – as well as tackling whole team interaction issues and finding new ways to get the parts and the whole to be all they can be. Your strategies, actions and behaviours on a daily basis have a marked impact on your team, and the better you are, the better your team will be. This is the book to help you raise your performance management ability.

Managing for Performance is designed to be a constant source of reference throughout your career whether you are a seasoned manager wanting to refresh and refocus your approach, or a new team leader just starting out. It provides ideas, tips and techniques to assist you in selecting the right approach, and will help you to deal with some of the tricky situations you may face.

Do you want to:

- Develop your leadership capability?
- Understand how to motivate your people?
- Develop the potential in your team?
- Turn around poor performance?
- Enhance your skills in coaching?
- Learn the secrets of effective delegating?
- Develop your emotional intelligence?
- Manage effective performance reviews?
- Make the right selection decisions?

- Manage conflict effectively?
- Work with people from different cultures and backgrounds?
- Understand how to manage upwards and be influential in your organisation?
- Work with multiple stakeholders to achieve results?

If the answer to at least five of these questions is YES then you will find plenty here to help you.

The list above should not be a welcome addition in your repertoire of skills. It is a MUST HAVE.

There is now ample evidence that the people skills of a manager are reflected directly in bottom line performance. It's obvious really; a more motivated team is much more likely to go the extra mile and deliver customer satisfaction. It is also clear that your emotional intelligence is a key aspect of successful leadership, so focusing on these skills and techniques could enhance your leadership profile.

Reflecting on how you are managing your people is not just important for your success and that of your organisation, but for your own work-life balance. With increasing pressures, competing demands and more complex team structures you need to be able to delegate and develop your team to take on greater responsibility. This doesn't happen overnight. It takes time, effort and understanding both of yourself and others to achieve the balance you are probably looking for.

Who is this book for?

This book will be of value to you if you are:

- An established manager or team leader wanting to hone and develop your skills.
- A new manager, perhaps realising that managing the performance of your team isn't quite as easy as you imagined.

- Someone who does not directly manage others but still has to motivate, influence and ensure that the people you work with deliver quality results.
- Working in the area of management development and are looking for new ways of helping managers and their teams work more effectively together.

It will help you to act as your own coach, developing the skills and techniques to meet the challenge of managing people and performance in your own world of work.

How the book is organised

This book is divided into three parts which are clearly signposted so that you can easily find the topic and area you are interested in. It takes a pragmatic approach, blending the latest thinking with practical ideas and techniques. You will have the opportunity to assess your own approach, understand others and plan for virtually every interaction you may have with the individuals and teams you work with.

Part 1 – Getting the best from others

Part 1 focuses on getting the best out of the individuals you work with. It provides the opportunity to reflect on your own approach and understand more about how to motivate and help others to achieve success. You will be able to analyse your team, identify their personal motivational package and map the different aspects influencing motivation and success. You will have the chance to grapple with some widely held assumptions around the role of reward and motivation, and identify the tools that you have at your disposal to bring out the best in others. You will also learn how to manage the performance of the people you work with. The challenge of helping everyone in your team perform to their potential is not easy. The 4C's for performance will enable you to identify performance issues and rectify them before they become real problems so that you can constantly be working to bring out the best in your people.

Part 2 – Developing effective relationships

Building positive relationships and working effectively with others is an essential part of enhancing the performance and motivation of the people you work with. In Part 2 you will have the opportunity to assess your competency, learn how to enhance your emotional intelligence and understand more about how to relate effectively with others. You will also explore three of the most important techniques managers can use to enhance performance – coaching, feedback and delegation. Finally, this section will help you to apply the techniques and competencies to some everyday situations so that you get the best out of one-to-one conversations.

Part 3 – Building high-performing teams

Part 3 gives you the opportunity to analyse the type of team you are working with and explores the consequences of working in cross-cultural environments and in teams which are geographically dispersed. It will also help you to understand some of the reasons why teams fail to achieve their full potential.

Creating a high-performancing team doesn't happen by magic. It takes skill to develop a new team or turn round an existing one. The team tool kit introduced in Chapter 7 will provide you with a host of techniques and ideas you can use to establish clarity of purpose, manage performance, build trust and establish processes to work effectively together. You will be able to explore your role as a team leader and focus on how to develop and hone your leadership style. Going through a range of approaches you will learn how to adapt your style in order to bring out the best in your team. In addition, you will learn to lead upwards and outwards in the organisation so that you can work to secure the long-term success of your team.

Conclusion

The conclusion has been designed to help you to continue to grow and develop. It provides references, ideas for further reading and useful websites and resources to help you and your team on the path to high performance.

Author's Acknowledgement

As someone who has spent most of their career in the field of management development, there are so many people I would like to thank, who have over the years helped to develop my thinking and expertise.

At the forefront are many of my colleagues at Ashridge The Performance through People tutorial team for their creativity and challenge, Fiona Dent for her encouragement, Mary Kennedy for her support, Richard Phillips for the use of the cross cultural questionnaire, and Lorraine Oliver and Rachel Piper from the Ashridge Learning Resource Centre who have tracked down much of the reference and research material used.

The recent research work, which has influenced the later chapters in the book has greatly benefited from the expertise of Viki Holton, Principal Researcher Ashridge, Diana Roper from BT, Mark Fritz of *Procedor,* with his focus on outcome thinking, and Barbara Harvey from Accenture for her competence and enthusiasm in developing and working with teams.

The many client organisations and managers I have met, who have shared their stories and experiences, have all played a part in encouraging me to communicate my approach to managing performance.

I have greatly valued the support from the virtual team at Pearson, especially Rachael Stock and Samantha Jackson, who have guided me through the process so efficiently.

Finally a heart felt thanks goes to my husband Dave for all his technical, emotional and family support.

Dedicated to: Dave, Joshua and Emma.

1

Bringing Out the Best in Others

Bringing out the best in others

A more motivated team is one that will put in extra effort to achieve customer satisfaction. It will be committed to delivering quality results and more inclined to achieve success. This section will explore motivation from a number of different angles. As a manager your approach has the potential to bring out the best in the team and, of course, the worst. So developing greater awareness of your impact on others is an important starting place. It also provides some frameworks and approaches to help you appreciate differences in your team – that people will have their own personal package of values and motivations. Once you understand this you are in a better position to adapt your style and approach in order to motivate them to achieve their best.

Along with understanding the role of motivation, you also need to be equipped with skills and techniques to work with some of the more difficult performance issues you face. Chapter 2 will help you focus on the issues in your team, recognise the reasons for a drop in performance, and take action to rectify the situation.

1

Motivating for Success

Does your style bring out the best in all of your team members, or does it have the potential to dilute their efforts?

Are you leading and managing your team in a way which encourages and inspires or does your approach dampen creativity and initiative?

Your Approach

Understanding motivation starts with understanding yourself.

As a manager you have an enormous impact on the motivation and attitude of your people. The more you can understand about yourself and your influence on others, the easier it will be for you to adapt your approach and improve your role as a manager. Understanding the assumptions you hold about others, your attitude and your behaviour will help you to understand the impact you have.

Identifying your assumptions

This self-assessment questionnaire, will tell you something about the type of manager you are and uncover some of the values and assumptions you hold about people. It is based on the work of the early motivational theorist, Douglas McGregor.

Below are 10 sets of paired statements. Please allocate 10 points per pair of statements. For example, if you agree much more with the first statement then allocate 8 points to that one and 2 to the second statement .

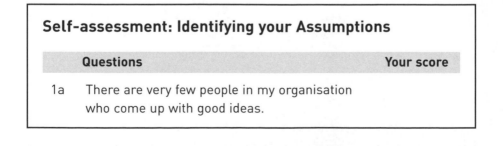

Self-assessment: Identifying your Assumptions	
Questions	**Your score**
1a There are very few people in my organisation who come up with good ideas.	

Questions	Your score

1b   Given the chance, most people in my organisation will come up with good ideas.

2a   The majority of people in my organisation prefer to be given direction.

2b   The majority of people in my organisation can and do exercise self-control and self-direction.

3a   People in my organisation do not have enough experience to offer practical ideas.

3b   Getting people to contribute ideas leads to the development of useful suggestions.

4a   For a manager to admit that an employee is right and they are wrong weakens their status among other employees.

4b   The manager's respect and reputation are enhanced by admitting to their mistakes.

5a   Paying people enough for the job means that they are less bothered with responsibility and recognition.

5b   A job that is challenging and interesting can go a long way in eradicating complaints about pay and benefits.

6a   If employees set their own standards, they tend to be lower than those set by the manager.

6b   If employees are allowed to set their own objectives and standards of performance, they tend to set them higher than their manager would.

7a   The more a person knows about the job and is free to make decisions about it, the more you have to keep an eye on them to keep them in line.

7b   Knowledge of the job and freedom to make decisions means fewer controls are needed to ensure competent performance.

8a   In the workplace people do not use imagination and inventiveness because they do not have much of either.

8b   The restrictions imposed by the job limit the ability of people to show imagination and creativity.

Questions	Your score
9a Quality tends to fall off when it is not supervised and imposed on people.	
9b When responsible for their own quality, people tend to raise their own standards.	
10a When there is bad news about the organisation, employees prefer the manager to keep it to themselves until it needs to be broken.	
10b Truth is better than fiction and most people prefer the full story no matter whether bad or good.	

Adapted from Paton and McCalman, *Change Management*, Sage Publications, 2006.

Add up the total scores for all the 'a' statements. This is your X score; 100 − your X score = your Y score, e.g. if your X score was 43, your Y score will be 57.

A high X score implies that you are someone who views employees as people who require direction, avoid responsibility and need to be controlled and managed.

A high Y score implies that you are someone who assumes that employees can be trusted and that they have the potential to contribute to a higher level of performance without being micro-managed.

Your Y score should be higher than your X score to fit into today's environment. When managers are operating at a distance from their team they have to develop a high level of trust and delegate responsibility in terms of outcomes rather than constantly check on the achievement of specific activities.

Remember behaviour breeds behaviour, and if you act as if you don't trust your people and feel the need to control them, the chances are that they will meet your expectations and will wait to be told what to do.

In creating a motivational environment ensure that your assumptions and presuppositions about people are more in line with the 'b' statements. If you expect good performance and encourage people's involvement and ideas, they will be more likely to take responsibility and demonstrate initiative.

Behaviours that Help

Your assumptions and attitudes drive your behaviour. Your beliefs often lead to 'self-fulfilling prophecies' – what you expect is what you get. Your everyday approach will have an effect on your team. But how do you know what will encourage good performance?

Think about managers you have had who have motivated you to work well and go that extra mile. Tick off the attitudes and behaviours from Table 1.1 that have influenced your behaviour and add your own descriptors.

Table 1.1 Attitudes and behaviours which lead to greater motivation

Attitudes which Lead to Greater Motivation	Behaviours which Lead to Greater Motivation
■ Trust.	■ Set clear objectives.
■ Honesty.	■ Had high expectations.
■ Openness.	■ Expected good performance.
■ Interest in me as a person.	■ Demonstrated commitment
■ Challenging.	through their own approach to
■ Encouraging.	work.
■ Straightforward.	■ Provided regular feedback.
■ Valued others.	■ Praised good performance.
■ Confidence.	■ Coached and developed.
■ Fairness and integrity.	■ Listened to ideas.
	■ Demonstrated an interest.
	■ Celebrated success.
	■ Encouraged me to take responsibility.
	■ Provided support and guidance.
	■ Encouraged my development.
	■ Reviewed my performance on a regular basis.

This list has been drawn up from talking to managers and finding out what works for them. There is also some interesting research which demonstrates that if you develop these skills, behaviours and attitudes, the chances are that not only will you motivate your people, but you will have an impact on the bottom line performance of your organisation.

This research was completed by Gallup organisation's Marcus Buckingham and Curt Coffman who worked with 25 years of interview data from over 1 million employees. The research described in their book *First, Break All The Rules* identified 12 of the survey questions which were linked directly to profit, productivity, employee retention and customer satisfaction.

The 12 Questions that Matter

1. Do I know what is expected of me at work?
2. Do I have the materials and equipment I need to do my work right?
3. At work, do I have the opportunity to do what I do best every day?
4. In the last seven days, have I received recognition or praise for doing good work?
5. Does my supervisor, or someone at work, seem to care about me as a person?
6. Is there someone at work who encourages my development?
7. At work, do my opinions seem to count?
8. Does the mission/purpose of my company make me feel my job is important?
9. Are my co-workers committed to doing quality work?
10. Do I have a best friend at work?
11. In the last six months, has someone at work talked to me about my progress?
12. This last year, have I had opportunities at work to learn and grow?

Case study

Best Buy is a consumer electronics speciality retailer in the US. In 1997 over 300 employees in different store locations were surveyed using the 12 questions. The employees were asked to give a

1–5 rating on the questions and the results showed that the scores were 60% higher in the most productive stores (those with the best retention rates, highest profits, etc). In fact employees in the most productive stores typically gave higher marks to all 12 questions than employees in the least productive stores. 'You take the same company, the same system and basically the same pay scale, and yet you get tremendously different attitudes among employees from different stores,' says Brad Anderson, president and COO of Best Buy, in an interview published in Fast Magazine. *'The only logical answer is leadership. We knew that the human side mattered, but these questions helped us understand just how it mattered. Someone who is gifted as a manager knows how to unlock the skill sets of people who work in that environment.'*

So unlocking the motivation in others is very much influenced by your approach. Why don't you ask your team to score the 12 questions on a 1–5 scale and see if you can do anything to help your people achieve their potential?

Here are some tips and ideas to help you hone your approach to motivating and understanding others. How many of these do you do?

Tips for Success

Tips	If you are satisfied that you are doing this give yourself a tick	If you think you should do this more often, make a note so that you can put the new behaviour into action
Walk the talk – show an interest in people and give them some time. If you can't see people face-to-face, call them on a regular basis.		

Tips	If you are satisfied that you are doing this give yourself a tick	If you think you should do this more often, make a note so that you can put the new behaviour into action
Praise people when you see a change or improvement.		
Provide regular, balanced feedback mixing positive messages with areas for improvement.		
Ask people what motivates them.		
Let people have ownership of what they do.		
Allow people to develop in their job.		
Reward good performance – remember rewards may not always be financial – praise, time off, recognition, a good appraisal, visibility with senior management, team events all count.		
Celebrate success with the whole team.		

Tips	If you are satisfied that you are doing this give yourself a tick	If you think you should do this more often, make a note so that you can put the new behaviour into action
Build a sense of team – good team work usually leads to high motivation.		
Help people to see how they fit in to the bigger picture.		
Set targets that are challenging but achievable.		
Ensure that the work environment is conducive to good performance – small changes can motivate people.		
Be positive – your approach will impact motivation of the team.		
Give people variety and interest and some control over what they do.		
Show that you trust your people.		
Provide training and development opportunities.		

Tips	If you are satisfied that you are doing this give yourself a tick	If you think you should do this more often, make a note so that you can put the new behaviour into action
If someone appears demotivated, talk to them about it.		
Involve people in decision making.		

Identify three things that you could do more of to create a more motivational work environment and set yourself an objective to achieve them.

1. _____
2. _____
3. _____

Understanding Others – Releasing Potential

It is often suggested that as a manager you should motivate your people. This implies that the motivation of your people is under your control. However, you can't force people to be motivated; motivation needs to come from within. Your role is to provide the conditions and environment where your people can and want to work to their potential.

One of the ways you can most easily create the conditions in which your team will want to work to their best is to make sure you understand what drives them. Don't assume that they have the same motivating factors as you. If you don't understand the individuals you are working with you will find it difficult to tap into their personal motivators and encourage higher performance.

Have you ever had any of these thoughts?

- I don't know what planet they are on.
- I wish I knew what made them tick.
- They are really capable but somehow don't seem switched on.
- My team members are so different from me.
- In my day things were different; we kept our heads down and just did a good job.
- People seem to want different things out of work – they don't seem to have the right attitude these days.

If so, you'll definitely benefit from the following quick briefing on how to understand what makes some people tick, and how to work out the mindset and motivating factors for those around you. Given that probably everyone in your team is different from you, this requires the ability to understand them, their values, life stages, and expectations from work.

LifeStyles and Life Stages

Expectations of work have changed greatly over the past decades. As job security has decreased and new ways of working are coming to the fore, the psychological contract between the organisation and employee has changed. Table 1.2 illustrates the change and highlights that what may have motivated people in the past may not be what motivates today.

This change has consequences for the organisation, and also for you as a manager as it is much more important now to find out what people want from work, and how you can help them to develop and combine their more individualistic needs with the needs of the organisation. In addition to these changes brought about by the economic environment, you also need to reflect on some of the socio-demographic data.

The people you work with will be made up of 'baby boomers', Generation X and Generation Y, and their different life experiences influence their approach to employment (note: Generations X and Y have no relationship to McGregor's X and Y on page 4)

Table 1.2 Past and present motivational factors

From the Old Contract	To the New Contract
Loyalty to the company.	Commitment to the current project.
Working towards a golden handshake.	Individual employee works as if self-employed.
Large traditional companies offering automatic promotion.	Companies strive to become employer of choice.
Employment for life.	Employability.
Pay based on seniority/longevity.	Pay based on contribution.
Regular promotion up the functions.	Variety and challenge across functions.
Incentives based on level and status (larger office/car, etc.).	Incentives based on personal reputation and expertise, team working and challenging projects.

Look at Table 1.3. Which are you? Can you identify your team members? Do the comments below ring true and if so, what are the consequences?

The concept of Generations X and Y and baby boomers is culturally specific to some of the western world. However, it is well worth reflecting on the history and socio-economic changes of the country and people you are working with and thinking about their implications in order to understand more about the expectations and motivational drivers of the team you work with.

Tapping into the socio-economic and demographic background of colleagues can provide some insight into their values and motivators. So too can understanding the life stages they are going through. Setting up home, having a family, etc. all influence the motivations and aspirations people hold. Some organisations have recognised this by implementing flexible contracts and working hours. Others have taken the approach of adopting a flexible benefit approach, whereby people can tailor the types of benefits available to their specific needs or life stage.

Table 1.3 Life experience and approach to employment

Baby Boomers Born between 1946 and 1961	Generation X Born between 1962 and 1977	Generation Y Born between 1978 and 1994
Like stability and predictability.	Achievement-oriented entrepreneurs.	High level of confidence and self-esteem.
Loyal to one organisation for most of their career.	Experienced their parents' redundancies so are less loyal to one organisation.	Technologically literate and have different ways of learning and assimilating information.
Corporation men/women – do what is asked.	Independent (latchkey kids).	Need constant stimulation – get bored easily.
Enjoy the security and the idea of 'a job for life'.	Realistic – have seen economic downturn.	High ambitions – expect good salaries and promotion early on.
Have a strong work ethic.	Performance oriented – are keen to learn.	Want work-life balance and expect it.
		Frustrated at organisations and their dead wood.

Whilst you may not have the power to influence the human resource systems in your organisation, by understanding something about your people, their life stage and aspirations you will be able to understand a little more about what currently motivates them, and tailor your approach accordingly

The Personal Package

In addition to thinking about life stages it is important to have some understanding of people's underlying values, what makes them 'tick'.

We all have a different package of motivational drivers. This affects how you work and the level of satisfaction you achieve. Some of these drivers will probably be part of your overall personal package throughout life or, as we have seen, be influenced by your current life stage.

Use the Self-assessment framework to identify your own package. Tick the drivers which relate to you. Your personal package may be made up from a combination of different factors. If your motivational needs and drivers are being met, the chances are that you are satisfied with your role and are working well, delivering results and perhaps going that extra mile.

However, if your personal package is not aligned with your role and the way you are being motivated and managed, the chances are that you are not working to your true potential. The same will be true for your team, so we will be using this framework to look at how you can help them to achieve their potential.

Self-assessment The Personal Package

Personal Drivers	Descriptor	What Motivates	What Demotivates
Independence	■ People who enjoy freedom and autonomy. ■ They will like to define their pace of work and how they develop their role. ■ They may show their autonomy in developing their own style. ■ They probably won't like working regular office hours or being desk bound.	■ Being independent. ■ The ability to set their own pace at work. ■ Few restrictions and rules. ■ Trust and freedom to develop their role. ■ Freedom to dress and work in their own style. ■ Flexible benefits. ■ Flexible ways of working. ■ Portable forms of recognition which enhance their autonomy further.	■ Constant checking. ■ Restrictions to their freedom. ■ Rigid structures and systems.

Personal Drivers	Descriptor	What Motivates	What Demotivates
Materialism	■ People who are concerned with developing wealth and improving their life style. ■ They are interested in monetary recognition. ■ They may be talking about their home/holidays/ recent purchases. ■ They may be aspirational, seeing their future in terms of material benefits. ■ They may also demonstrate conspicuous consumption i.e. car/clothing, jewellery	■ Monetary reward, bonuses or the idea of a swift promotion route. ■ Fringe benefits such as car allowance will be important. ■ A role which has a direct link between performance and monetary reward.	■ Lack of financial recognition or a career path which can match their aspirations.
Influence	People who like to influence the way others behave. ■ They may like to manage others and take a lead in managing projects and initiatives. ■ They like to make things happen through others.	■ Responsible, challenging work with leadership requirements. ■ The ability to influence others and manage change. ■ The ability to make a difference.	■ Not being listened to. ■ Not having the opportunity to use their ability to influence.

Personal Drivers	Descriptor	What Motivates	What Demotivates
Recognition	■ People who are motivated by praise. ■ They react well to praise. ■ They may also be good at giving praise to others.	■ Regular feedback. ■ Recognition from customers or others in the organisation. ■ Being recognised in team meetings for achievements. ■ Receiving awards or tokens of appreciation. ■ An email saying 'Thanks'.	■ Working in an environment where praise and feedback is not evident.
Organisation	■ People with this driver are motivated by a need for structure and order. ■ They may appear organised at work – clear desk etc, and systematic in their approach. ■ They may not want to take risks without weighing up the consequences.	■ A role where they can use their skills. ■ A degree of stability in their role. ■ A degree of job security. ■ Clear objectives and career paths. ■ The opportunity to create a new structure.	■ Disorganisation. ■ Constant change. ■ Changing goalposts. ■ Lack of clarity around rewards and recognition.

Personal Drivers	Descriptor	What Motivates	What Demotivates
Victory	▪ People who like overcoming challenges and obstacles. ▪ They enjoy achieving results. ▪ They may be competitive. ▪ They demonstrate energy to achieve their goal.	▪ The challenge itself is the overriding motivator and the opportunity to succeed. ▪ Recognition for achievement is important. ▪ The freedom to focus on the challenge at hand.	▪ Literally lack of challenge. ▪ Lack of recognition for achievement. ▪ Administration and red tape which will get in the way.
Expertise	▪ People who like to be an expert in their field. ▪ The content of the work is what inspires them.	▪ Work that challenges their skills. ▪ Autonomy and facilities to deliver results. ▪ The opportunity to use their specialist skills. ▪ Professional recognition	▪ Administration. ▪ Promotion if it takes them away from their expertise.

Personal Drivers	Descriptor	What Motivates	What Demotivates
Relationships	■ People who value working with others. ■ They may be a team player. ■ They are usually good net workers. ■ They usually work in a friendly and supportive manner. ■ They don't usually like working alone.	■ The ability to work with others. ■ Working in a team to achieve results. ■ A customer facing role or role which involves working with others. ■ Team-based targets and rewards.	■ Lack of contact with others. ■ Working in a hostile or unfriendly environment. ■ Working alone for long periods of time.
Self-development	■ People who are motivated by learning, personal growth and development. ■ They may be attending courses outside work to develop. ■ They may enjoy working towards qualifications.	■ Jobs which provide the opportunity to develop new skills. ■ The ability to attend courses and gain qualifications. ■ On the job learning. ■ The opportunity for coaching and mentoring.	■ A role which does not allow for growth. ■ Lack of training and development. ■ Lack of support for their development.

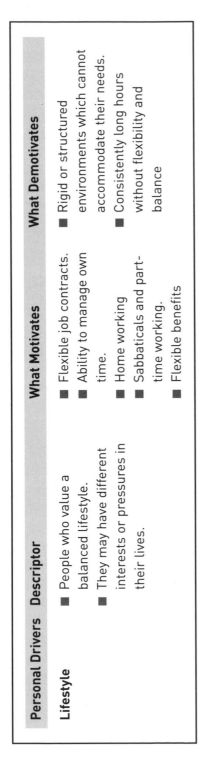

Personal Drivers	Descriptor	What Motivates	What Demotivates
Lifestyle	■ People who value a balanced lifestyle. ■ They may have different interests or pressures in their lives.	■ Flexible job contracts. ■ Ability to manage own time. ■ Home working ■ Sabbaticals and part-time working. ■ Flexible benefits	■ Rigid or structured environments which cannot accommodate their needs. ■ Consistently long hours without flexibility and balance

Putting the personal package to work

If you can identify other people's personal package you will be much more likely to know how to motivate them and identify the particular incentives and approaches you could use to help them achieve.

You can gather a lot of information about an individual by just chatting to them as you walk down the corridor, or talking over the phone. Simple questions such as asking about what they did at the weekend, or just casually enquiring how things are going with their job, can provide valuable information. This takes up time but understanding your team is an important part of your role and if you get it right the results should be evident.

You may want to use a few of the questions below in the performance review process. They should give you some insight into the person's motivational package:

- What do you like best about your job?
- What would make your job more satisfying?
- What are your aspirations for the future?
- What do you see yourself doing in five years?
- What do you definitely not want to see yourself doing in five years?

Here are a few case studies to illustrate just how important it is to tap into the needs and values of others.

Case study

Pete is an engineer. He has a degree and has been working for his current organisation for the past 10 years. He likes nothing better than to have the time and space to develop and work on new projects. He is particularly interested in the new computer systems and techniques which support his work. In fact, he often takes the software packages home to tinker about on his home computer with them. He loves the mathematical challenge of it all, but gets frustrated at times with the sales team who seem to change their mind about what they want. In addition, the procurement department always seem to want masses of paperwork from him. Whilst he is dedicated to his job, he has quite a few outside interests and likes to work regular hours so that he can manage his social commitments.

What do you think Pete's motivational package is?
As his manager, how could you encourage Pete to maintain and develop his motivation?

Pete's main drivers are his expertise and lifestyle. To encourage Pete his manager may want to think about the following:

- *Continuing to allow the space for Pete to develop the projects.*
- *Managing the interface with the sales and procurement department – perhaps helping Pete to find easier ways of meeting their requirements.*
- *Allowing Pete to attend a conference in his specialist area.*
- *Asking him to test out any new IT packages and provide some feedback on their usefulness to the department.*
- *Providing specific feedback on Pete's achievements.*
- *Taking an interest in the technical side of Pete's job.*

Case study

Sally has been working in the organisation for five years now. However, her timekeeping is slipping and she has been taking more time off sick than usual. Her boss has a chat with her and over a coffee discovers that Sally is frustrated. She feels she can do more and hates the restrictions of sitting at the computer all day. She feels she needs more of a challenge and would like to see a change in the way some of the systems and processes are working. In particular she is concerned that the organisation is missing out on some major opportunities to attract new customers. Sally would like to capitalise on these ideas, but her dissatisfaction is leading her to consider other jobs offering higher salaries and greater opportunity.

As her boss you have always been pleased with Sally's work but have been concerned that her current performance isn't up to its usual level.

What do you think Sally's motivational package consists of? As her manager, what could you do to improve things?

Sally has obviously gained confidence over the years and is discovering that the original job she applied for in the organisation is no longer matching her needs. She seems to be driven much more by challenge, change, achievement and reward which would imply that her drivers are around influence, challenge and material reward.

As such you may want to think about:

- *Letting Sally work on a project to improve the processes or attract new customers. This would be a good way of testing out whether her abilities match up to her aspirations. You would obviously need to support Sally with coaching and training if appropriate.*
- *Talking to Sally about possible future roles and identifying how she could go about preparing herself for a new role.*
- *Allowing Sally to shadow someone else in the organisation who is working in a more entrepreneurial role so that she can see if it is something she really aspires to.*
- *Looking at Sally's current job and seeing if there is any way the job could be enriched to meet her aspirations.*

The language of motivation

Once you have an idea of the motivators and drivers of your team members you can start to think about how you might approach them. The language of motivation is very important. How you present an idea to someone means that you could either inspire them to take on the task with enthusiasm or turn them right off.

Imagine that your team has been assigned a project which involves data collection and analysis. One of your team will need to be responsible for gathering customer data on some of your products. They will need to analyse the results and make recommendations to the production and sales team about how you can increase your current market share.

Think about how you could change your language to delegate the task to different people with different motivational drivers.

For example, if someone has a strong 'relationship' driver you would emphasise the importance of working with others, the opportunity to meet with customers and work across departments.

For someone with a victory driver, you would emphasise the challenge of delivering results, making a difference, getting recognition and achieving something of value for the organisation.

Table 1.4 gives an example of how you could rephrase the same message for different motivational types.

Table 1.4 Rephrasing the same message for different motivational types

Personal Driver	What You Might Say
Independence	This project will provide you with freedom to decide how to achieve the results. You'll have the opportunity to decide how to achieve the goal.
Materialism	This will influence your performance targets.
Influence	You will have the opportunity to influence the results. We need to convince others of the change needed.
Recognition	I know you are fully capable of achieving this. I really appreciate what you bring to the role.
Organisation	We have a clear goal to achieve. Let's set up some targets and review points.
Victory	This is a tough challenge but it will make a difference to the team.

Expertise	This project requires a lot of specialist knowledge.
	I really value what you can bring in terms of your expertise and background.
Relationships	You will have the opportunity to work across the organisation.
	We need to build relationships with X, Y and Z.
Self-development	I see this as a real opportunity to develop a greater understanding of the organisation.
Lifestyle	We need to achieve this by . . . and you can plan your time accordingly.

Creating a motivational map

Mind maps created by Tony Buzan are a fantastic way of visualising, creating and sorting information. They can be used to create a motivational map of your team and the people you work with.

All you need is a blank sheet of paper and some pens to get started.

- In the centre of the page draw a circle with an image to represent the team/department. Add main branches for each of your team (including yourself), identifying their name and role.
- Add smaller branches to identify their key tasks (or key result areas). You may want to indicate which areas of their job they are doing well and those in which they are not as successful.
- Add any information you may know about them – Generation X or Y, life stage, etc.
- Add each person's personal package of motivators.
- Identify and add their strengths (think about knowledge, skills and attitudes).
- Identify and add their areas for development (think about knowledge, skills and attitudes).

Once you've completed the mind map, consider the following questions.

- How well do you know your team?
- What else do you now know about them from completing this exercise?

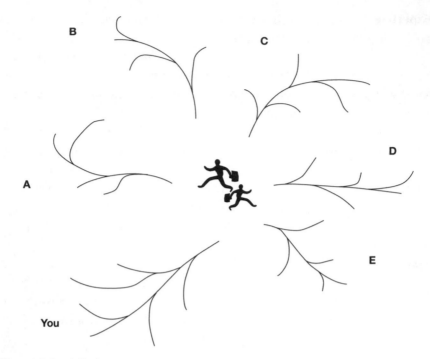

Figure 1.1 Mind map

- Do you treat all team members the same or recognise the differences? If so, how?
- What can you do differently to get the best from the individuals in your team?
- How can you work with their strengths and develop the weaker areas?

Self-assessment Team Motivation

Name	Your Analysis	Actions You Could Take to Enhance Motivation
Lifestyle and life stage		
Key motivators		
Strengths		
Development areas		
Any other information (aspirations/likes/dislikes)		

From the mind map exercise develop a motivational plan for each of your team, using the Self-assessment framework.

Once you have this information you can reflect on the types of motivators and rewards you can offer. Also, how might you want to frame or present ideas in a way that would get them to achieve their potential?

If you don't see your team on a regular basis, you can use team meetings to help build up a map. Make sure that you have sufficient time to build in opportunities to get to know the team. You may want to use the 12 questions or the personal package to generate a discussion around what motivates them as individuals and as a team or use one of the questionnaires recommended in the Conclusion.

Reward as a motivator

Reward is always associated with motivation, and often when we mention reward, people associate it with money – issues of salary, stock options, profit sharing and performance related pay.

Performance related pay (PRP) has been seen as the Holy Grail in managing performance, but it comes with a health warning. If it is not carefully managed, it can in fact become a demotivator. Look at the pros and cons listed in Table 1.5 and reflect on your own experience.

Research has shown that in certain jobs such as sales functions incentive schemes can work well, but when you compare this to other professions such as research science, public sector and non-profit sectors, you can see that it may not always work to great effect.

If you are working in an organisation where performance related pay is being used, here are a few tips to help you to implement it in a way which can continue to develop motivation amongst all team members.

■ Be fair – make sure that you are allocating incentives fairly amongst the team members. This means that you need a clear understanding of their performance and their contribution to achieving the results.

Table 1.5 Pros and cons of performance related pay

Pros	Cons
■ It can directly reward good performance.	■ What you measure and reward is what you get. As a result people may not focus on other areas of their job.
■ It works well in roles where results can be easily measured and monitored.	■ People come to associate performance with money so may not wish to go the extra mile if there is no reward.
■ It can be used effectively to reward team performance as well as individual performance.	■ Those who just miss their target can be very demotivated, especially if they feel they have performed well.
■ It can be used to reward tangible outputs as well as skills and competences.	■ Not all roles can be measured in such a direct cause-effect fashion.
■ It can create a clear differentiator between good performers and poor performers.	■ Other factors may influence performance – environmental circumstances/the input from others etc.
■ If people are motivated by financial reward it can work well.	■ Sometimes a focus on individual rewards can lead to competition and lack of team work.
■ If the rewards are achievable and worth aiming for, the approach is more likely to work	■ Often PRP is presented as a 'one size fits all' approach. Often the roles within one team or department are more varied than others.

- To accurately measure performance you will need to have clear objectives which are regularly monitored.
- See the bigger picture – understand the economic environment. Are all your team working on a level playing field?
- Understand who is involved – is success just down to the performance of one individual or was it a team effort?

■ Be clear with those who do not receive rewards. Tell them what they need to do to improve and be prepared to put in the time and effort to coach them to success.

■ Try to take into account the whole person – are they performing effectively in all areas of their job?

You might not have a great deal of influence over the financial aspect of reward but you do have influence over a whole array of rewards. These can offer a more flexible and effective approach, recognising good performance when you see it.

For individuals to be motivated, they need to have realistic objectives to strive for. They need to enjoy their job, and feel their work is recognised and appreciated. Small things such as praise, time off, new projects and development opportunities can be very effective and can also improve loyalty.

HR magazine highlighted some research from the US assessing employee recognition practices most valued by 750 employees across various industries that found that those ranked at the top involved no cost at all, with several of the top 10 involving praise rather than perks or gifts. The number one most important recognition from a manager was support and involvement, followed by personal praise and then autonomy and authority. Cash and other monetary awards came in at number 10

Summary

Helping to motivate your team is an important part of managing performance. To do this effectively you need to:

■ Understand yourself – your own assumptions and behaviours are important
■ Understand the values and drivers of your team members.
■ Adapt your approach to each team member.
■ Think about incentives and rewards you can offer in the light of individual differences.
■ Recognise that your role in motivating your team is not just a nice thing to do – it will have a direct impact on bottom line performance.

Managing Performance Difficulties

There are always people who present us with challenges. Often managers say they spend 80% of their time dealing with individuals who have performance issues and only 20% with the rest of their team. The key to success is to recognise and manage performance issues as efficiently as possible and, ideally, help stop people slipping into poor performance in the first place.

Look at Yourself – from Ostrich to Judge

Let's start with looking at your own approach to managing performance problems. Take a look at the caricatures below and see if you can recognise yourself in any of them.

The Ostrich

Do you put your head in the sand and hope that the problem will go away or perhaps go unnoticed? If so, beware. Performance problems build up and you can be sure that the team will be noticing the situation. This could affect team morale and your own credibility as a manager.

The Pass the Parcel Expert

Have you been guilty of getting rid of your problem by transferring the individual to another team or moving them to 'special projects'? This may seem an easy way out, but the cost to your reputation and to the organisation as a whole may be worth considering. You probably know how tough it is when the same thing happens to you, so consider tackling the issue rather than passing it on.

The Band-aid Worker

Are you good at listening and giving some time to your poor performers? Do you try various solutions and provide some support and development? This is all very admirable but there may be a point when you need to recognise that more is required. It may be worth delving into the real reasons for the performance issue: combining your support with a challenging development plan can facilitate change and improvement.

The Delegator

Have you ever been guilty of delegating performance issues to other people to manage? There is nothing wrong with this, providing that you are doing it for the right reason and not because you don't relish dealing with the problem yourself. If you do delegate the task to someone else, make sure that you provide sufficient support, coaching and guidance.

The Prejudger

Do you ever make snap decisions about people or jump to conclusions? This is not unusual. We often operate with a 'halo or horns' mentality, seeing people as either 'all good' or 'all bad' performers. Such labels are unhelpful and it may be worth checking out your perceptions with a range of people before you make any assumptions.

The 4 P's of Performance

Often poor performance is something that develops over time. If you can notice the drop-off in performance and act on it before it becomes a problem you have a greater opportunity to help turn the situation around.

Look at Figure 2.1.

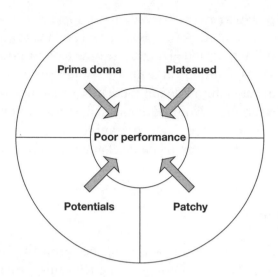

Figure 2.1   The four types of performance issues

It identifies the four types of performance issues which, if not managed well, could potentially move into the zone of poor performance and become a real issue:

1. Prima donna performer.
2. Plateaued performer.
3. Potential performer.
4. Patchy performer.

The four types of performance issues are described below with suggestions for how to tackle them.

1. Prima Donna Performers

All managers want people who are bright, energetic, take the initiative and go the extra mile. Our top performers are valuable but they can also demand extra attention and time in order to get the best out of them.

Often these people have strong motivators around achievement and challenge. They love being stretched, taking on more and feeling that they are progressing. They are career oriented, and hungry for new experiences. Generally, they will want to run with tasks and don't take kindly to micro-management.

This sounds fantastic but on the down side these people may be difficult to manage. Because they are quick thinkers, they may find it hard to bring others along with them. They may be difficult to pin down and guide in the direction you want them to go. If they are good at delivering results they may have bargaining power which they hold over you. In addition, they may have sacrificed developing some competencies such as team building and relationship management, leaving problems in their wake.

Case study

Paula is one of the top performers in the team. She always delivers results, takes risks and negotiates deals which mean that year-on-year she exceeds her targets. Her manager was initially very impressed with Paula and, because of her business success, allowed her to do her own thing and have more or less free rein, much to the annoyance of other team members. However, Paula is becoming more and more difficult to pin down. The paperwork associated with the role is never up to date and she is becoming more of a maverick, not contributing to the overall ethos of the team which is to work in a collaborative way, assisting each other and sharing information. Her manager feels guilty as this situation has developed partly because he does not know how to deal with Paula. Now he faces the challenge of bringing her performance back into line, but does not relish the conversation and, in addition, is afraid of jeopardising the business results.

This maverick approach is not unusual and is hard to tackle because of the personalities involved, combined with the fact that individual performance targets are being achieved.

A change in behaviour will only happen if there is an objective reason for the individual to continue to achieve and develop.

One of the concepts which often encourages talented mangers to sit up

Table 2.1 Skills associated with early and more senior leadership roles

Success in Early Management Positions is Often Associated with	Success in More Senior Leadership Positions is Often Associated with
Independence	Being a team player
Ability to control short-term	Having longer-term strategic vision
results	Managing the creativity of others
Creativity	Self-esteem
Ambition and high standards	General management skills
Speciality strength	Creating unity and cohesion
Being contentious – taking a stand	

and think is the threat of 'derailment', identified through research at the centre for Creative Leadership. The skills which help managers achieve success early on in their career can literally derail them as they move into more senior positions (see Table 2.1).

There are differences between successful managers and those that derail. The successful managers:

- Have more diversity in their track record
- Maintain composure under stress
- Handle mistakes with poise and grace
- Focus on problems and solve them
- Get along with all kinds of people

If you want to stop your prima donna performers peaking and becoming poor performers, it may be worth discussing the implications of derailment to them in the context of their own career progression.

In addition, it is important to keep your peak performers on track, encouraging their talents and helping them sustain and develop their potential for the future. You can achieve this by:

- Using 360° feedback as a tool for understanding and appreciating the need for broad leadership and team skills
- Measuring and rewarding performance on a range of competencies, not just business results. In many organisations, rewards and bonuses

are based on achievement against business **and** leadership competencies

- Understanding what motivates and drives them to work in this way
- Helping them to plan their career and identify the steps to success
- Secondments can help as a great way of getting extra experience and exposure and perhaps understanding their overall role in the organisation
- Encouraging them to take responsibility for their own career planning
- Involving them in development activities so that they are part of the solution
- Involving them in coaching and developing others as they have lots of experience to pass on
- Encouraging them to find a mentor who can advise and help them to develop further
- Being clear about what you need in terms of review, communication and feedback.
- Providing a climate where challenge and learning is encouraged

2. Plateaued Performers

Often these are the most difficult people to work with. They are not exactly poor performers but they are not achieving their potential and are ticking over doing the bare minimum.

Like any performance situation it's important to find out the reasons behind their approach.

Is it that:

- Their previous manager didn't have any expectations of them?
- They are dissatisfied with the way they have been treated in the past?
- They are afraid of change and perhaps finding it hard to adapt to new technology?
- They are coasting into retirement?
- They are lacking in confidence, perhaps feeling inadequate as new people with new ideas join the business?
- They have other things going on in their lives and work is not their main focus?
- They are stuck in their comfort zone?

You need to decide if this level of performance is acceptable. Can you afford to accommodate plateaued performers in your team? What is the impact on the business? What is the impact on the individual, and what is the impact on the overall team? What is the impact on you as a manager and team leader? Is your credibility at stake?

Having thought through these questions you are probably aware that not taking action can have huge consequences.

Look at the case study below.

Case study

Tim had been working with the company for a number of years. Initially he had shown spark and enthusiasm but now just did exactly what was asked and no more. Whenever his boss tried to delegate activities there was always some excuse and the work was never really up to standard. The rest of the team seemed to be shouldering the burden as gradually people had stopped asking Tim for help because they knew it would probably not be forthcoming. Even other departments chose to contact Tim's colleagues because they knew they would get a better level of service from them.

So what action could Tim's boss take?

Doing nothing is an easy way out but would have major consequences for team performance and morale.

- *The first step would be to have a conversation. Is Tim aware of the impact of his behaviour? What motivates him in his work? What is he good at? What does he struggle with?*
- *What might be the reasons for the drop in performance?*
- *Is there anything Tim is good at or enthusiastic about?*
- *Put him alongside a more enthusiastic member of the team.*
- *Make him aware of the consequences of his performance and set a clear monitored development plan.*

- *Set objectives which are specifically focused on improving performance.*
- *As Tim is experienced, involve him in coaching new members of the team.*
- *Provide appropriate development and secondment to other areas if you think this will remotivate him.*
- *Show that you value him and expect good performance.*
- *Try to understand what motivates him – he performed well in the past so should be able to perform well in the future.*
- *Find out 'what's in it for him' – what will motivate him to perform at a higher level.*

If these approaches don't work it will be important to develop an improvement plan and monitor progress, as plateaued performers can soon turn into poor performers.

3. Potential Performers

The potential performers are the people in your team who are keen and enthusiastic. They have potential to go further in the organisation. Often these people get the least attention as they continually do a good job and take up little of your time. Yet these individuals are the gems which need to be nurtured and developed and will benefit from your advice, guidance and coaching.

The message with your potentials is, 'Don't ignore them'. You will also probably get a great deal of satisfaction from watching them grow and develop and the chances are that if you get a reputation as a good people developer you will probably attract more high-potential people to your team. The old adage that managers get the people they deserve could not be more appropriate in this situation.

Case study

Pat was someone who always did a great job. She was prepared to stay late when needed and always had time to help others in the team. She was a quick learner and had come up with new ideas and processes. Her manager appreciated the fact that she was so efficient and enthusiastic and often gave her extra tasks to complete. Pat, however, was beginning to feel frustrated. She knew she could do more and wanted to take extra qualifications. She had decided that if she didn't progress further in the next year she would look elsewhere to develop her career.

Pat's manager obviously appreciates her work and seems willing to encourage her development and would need to discuss:

- *Her long-term development. Where does she see herself going in the future?*
- *What development does she need?*
- *How can they meet both the department's needs and her own individual needs?*
- *How can they pace her development and provide sufficient experience and exposure?*
- *Is there any area of her work which would benefit from coaching?*
- *Are there any projects or tasks which could be delegated to her?*
- *How can they manage the more mundane parts of her role?*

It is important to recognise that if high-potential individuals go unrecognised, they won't hang around. They may either get frustrated and slip into the realms of poor performance or they may look elsewhere for challenge and development. Equally it is important to be clear about time scales and look at how to provide the variety and depth to prepare these people for their next role.

4. Patchy Performers

Patchy performers may often go unnoticed. They are people whose performance may vary during the year, or alternatively they may be good in some areas of their work but poor in others. As a result the severity of the situation may be overlooked. However, it is important to understand what is going on and identify the consequences, not just for the individual's current role but also for any future development they may wish to undertake.

Case study

Philip has been working in the team for a couple of years. At times his manager is really pleased with his performance. He generally produces good work and is a popular member of the team. However on occasions his performance is erratic. Sometimes reports are late and sometimes he does not follow up with clients. His manager is not always around as her team is spread over a number of sites. This means that she finds it difficult to understand what is going on and wonders whether she is missing anything else.

Philip's manager will need to:

■ *Set up a review to discuss the situation and discover why his performance is so patchy.*
■ *As she is not always around it is useful to gain feedback from other managers or people she can trust who may have more contact with Philip*
■ *Identify the reasons for patchy performance and any development needed*
■ *Depending on those reasons, Philip and his manager will need to identify a possible solution (this may be training, coaching, a change in roles and responsibilities, or clearer objectives and targets)*
■ *Regular reviews will be required to monitor progress and ensure that all aspects of performance are in line.*

The secret to managing patchy performers is regular and thorough reviews. These need to focus on specific objectives and competencies associated with the role. Understanding the reasons for the variances in performance is important. It is also important to understand the motivations and reasons for the instances of good performance. Once these issues have been recognised and understood, it will be essential to set up development and coaching to fill any gaps in capability and knowledge. It may also be worth reviewing the individual's role so they can focus on areas where their performance excels. Follow-up reviews should monitor progress and ensure that the individual is performing at a more consistent level throughout the year.

Managing Performance at a Distance

If you are managing the performance of people you don't see on a regular basis you need to make sure that you set up processes and means of monitoring performance and ensure that you are able to pick up on any potential issues as soon as possible.

- Make sure you set up a clear contract with team members around the outcomes and deliverables you expect
- Have regular telephone meetings to check progress
- Make sure that there are clear measurement systems so that you can track progress
- Use 360° feedback to highlight strengths and potential issues
- Don't just contact people when there are problems
- Remember to praise good performance as this encourages people to do more.
- Create connections across the team so people understand how their role fits in with others
- Have people on the ground who can give you feedback on progress and development
- Help people to see the big picture so that they can see where their contribution fits in.

How to Deal with Performance Problems

The examples above are focused on how to keep performance on track and prevent it from becoming a more entrenched issue. However, you may be experiencing this problem now. In these cases ask yourself:

- Do you know what is causing the problem?
- What action have you taken?

These two questions are the keys to managing underperformance. The first step is to understand 'why', and the second is to 'take action' as soon as possible to rectify the situation.

Why Performance Deteriorates

The worst thing you can do is to ignore underperformance. It's almost like thinking of sand falling through an hour glass. If you can catch the grains as they fall through there is less work to do later. Letting the sand continue will only lead to a build up which takes longer to reverse.

If someone's performance has deteriorated the first thing to do is to look at the possible reasons for it. These are summarised in Figure 2.2.

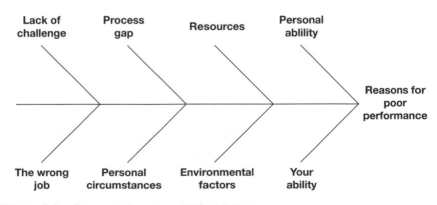

Figure 2.2 Reasons for poor performance

Look at the list of possible reasons in the Self-assessment box and think about their relevance to any poor performers you may have on your team.

Self-assessment Reasons for Poor Performance

Reasons

1. **Personal ability**
   Has the individual the capability to complete the task? Is there a gap between the task and the level of skills and competency of the person?

2. **Your ability**
   Have you given enough direction and clearly explained what you expect in terms of the standard of work?

3. **Resources**
   Are there adequate resources available?

4. **Environmental forces**
   Is the work environment creating difficulties either because of physical conditions, red tape or politics?

5. **Process gap**
   Has the appraisal system been at fault? Have the goalposts moved or external forces made them unobtainable? Have there been regular enough review sessions, and is the reward system pointing in the right direction?

6. **Personal circumstances**
   Has something happened in their personal life which is affecting their performance?

7. **Lack of challenge**
   Lack of challenge can be as harmful as too much challenge in the job.

8. **The wrong job**
   Sometimes people underperform because they are in a role which does not suit their skills and competencies. This can cause a lot of stress both for themselves and those around them.

Once you have identified the causes for the deterioration in performance, it is far easier to work on a joint solution and way forward.

If you can't identify any possible causes for the performance issue, it is important that you don't avoid the situation. Talk to the individual and if necessary involve your HR department.

Taking the Right Action

The first step is identifying the issue and once this has been achieved you can work on potential solutions (see Table 2.2).

Table 2.2 Reasons for deterioration in performance and possible solutions

Reasons	Possible Solutions
1. Personal ability Has the individual the capability to complete the task? Is there a gap between the task and the level of skills and competency of the person?	■ Set a clear development plan which will include training and coaching to rectify the situation. ■ Let the individual shadow or work alongside someone who is good at this particular skill. ■ Set some improvement objectives so that you can monitor performance and development. ■ Look at what they do well. Perhaps they are in the wrong job and may excel doing something else.
2. Your ability Have you given enough direction and clearly explained what you expect in terms of the standard of work?	■ Obtain feedback on your performance from others. ■ Keep a shared written agreement of action. ■ Confirm instructions and objectives in writing. ■ Make sure you don't give confusing messages.

Table 2.2 continued

Reasons	Possible Solutions
	■ Adjust your style.
	■ Ask the individual what you could do differently.
3. Resources Are there adequate resources available?	■ Can you help the person acquire resources?
	■ Can you help them present a case for more resources?
	■ Is there any way the current resources can be used more effectively.
	■ Make sure objectives are realistic.
4. Environmental forces Is the work environment creating difficulties either because of physical conditions, red tape or politics?	■ Identify the problem and look at what you can do together to rectify it.
	■ Help to change the work environment.
	■ Help to remove or manage the red tape and politics.
5. Process gap Has the appraisal system been at fault? Have the goalposts moved or external forces made them unobtainable? Have there been regular enough review sessions, and is the reward system pointing in the right direction?	■ Ensure that you hold regular reviews.
	■ Review goals in the light of changing circumstances.
	■ Be clear about their objectives and what you expect from them.
	■ Try to sort out any anomalies in the reward system.
6. Personal circumstances Has something happened in their personal life which is affecting their performance?	■ Spend time with the person to understand their problems and develop an action plan which will help them get back on track.
	■ Do they need time off work to sort the problem out?

Table 2.2 continued

Reasons	Possible Solutions
	■ Do they need to see an expert? Remember you are not expected to be a professional counsellor.
	■ Show empathy, but be clear about the consequences of poor performance.
	■ Set review meetings to monitor progress and reassess the situation on a regular basis.
7. Lack of challenge Lack of challenge can be as harmful as too much challenge in the job.	■ Look at ways of expanding their responsibility.
	■ Help them to prepare for the next step.
	■ Delegate to them, but give them recognition for the extra work.
	■ Are there any projects they could take on?
	■ Set challenging objectives.
	■ Discuss their future and what motivates them.
8. The wrong job Sometimes people underperform because they are in a role which does not suit their skills and competencies. This can cause a lot of stress both for themselves and those around them.	■ Agree the reason for underperformance and work on finding a joint solution.
	■ Identify their skills and look at whether there is another role they could take on.
	■ Is there any training they could do?
	■ Work on a plan for the future which may involve leaving the department or even organisation.
	■ Look at how you may use their strengths and abilities.

Once you have agreed that there is a need to focus on improving performance it is important to set some clear, measurable actions. These need to be agreed, put in writing and monitored on a regular basis. They also need to be supported by regular coaching and feedback.

Here are a few golden rules to help in the process:

- *Tackle performance issues immediately. Don't let them build into bigger problems.*
- *Be clear about the consequences of poor performance.*
- *Show that you expect good performance from everyone.*
- *Listen to reasons for poor performance but don't accept excuses, and be sure to leave the meeting with an agreed plan for improvement.*
- *Keep written notes so that you can both monitor progress.*
- *Don't label someone as a poor performer – labels stick and are not helpful.*

The Last Resort

If you have tried everything but feel that no progress has been made, it is important to then involve your HR department (if you have one). Under government legislation there needs to be evidence that the individual has been given every opportunity to improve. This means that you will need to develop and produce documented performance improvement plans over a reasonable period of time (Your HR department should be able to provide specific information on this). If there is no marked and sustained improvement it may then be appropriate to follow a disciplinary procedure, and again your HR department should be able to provide support and advice.

So, if you have reached a situation where you have advanced to a disciplinary procedure:

- Involve your HR department early on.
- Speak with your boss, as their support will be important.
- Make sure that you have kept written copies (which have been agreed by both parties) of all the appraisal and performance review meetings.
- Obtain feedback from other relevant people – 360° feedback can be

useful here and also feedback from other departments the individual may work with.

■ Show that you have been working on a development plan with the individual (again keep written copies of any information and plans that you have agreed).

■ Make sure that you get the support you need. At this stage it is often useful to have someone from the HR department to attend any meeting between yourself and the individual concerned.

Hopefully you won't have to resort to such measures and you can catch the performance slippage before it becomes a major difficulty for all concerned. But if this does happen, it is important to show that as a manager you have done everything you can to rectify the situation.

Taking Stock of Your Team

Take a few minutes to think about your team using the Self-assessment framework on the next page. Rate their performance on a scale of 1 to 10. Consider how you would like them to develop their performance and what actions you might need to take to help them achieve this.

Self-assessment Considering Your Team

Name	Rate performance on a 1 to 10 scale where 10 is excellent	Are they a 'P'? Prima donna Plateaued Potential Patchy Poor performer	Identify where the individual needs to focus to improve and develop their performance	Identify what actions you need to take

Summary

To get the best out of your team you need to recognise performance issues that people may be facing and work together to tackle them before they become real problems.

Remember:

- Think about whether your own approach might be part of the problem
- Uncover possible reasons behind performance issues
- Make sure you've accurately identified the type of potential performance problem you're dealing with and that you are taking the right action to overcome it
- Know what to do in the last resort
- Take stock of your team and identify how to help everyone achieve to their potential

2

Building Effective Relationships

Building Effective Relationships

Building effective relationships is a vital ingredient in managing perform-ance and delivering results, yet we often have little time to spend face-to-face with people at work. Emotional intelligence plays a crucial role here too and is a prerequisite for anyone wanting to develop their skills in working with others. Linked closely to this are the skills of lis-tening, questioning and building rapport – the bedrocks of any productive conversation. Used effectively these techniques can be used to create good relationships and deliver performance.

This chapter covers all the component parts of building effective relation-ships and shows you how to apply them to a whole range of conversations including performance reviews, selection interviews, counselling and coaching discussions. As you read on, you will realise that there is far more to building effective relationships than you might imagine and, whether you are working face-to-face with people or on a virtual basis, these skills are important in helping you build trust and understanding.

Core Competences and Skills

Core competence → Key skills → Essential techniques → Practical application

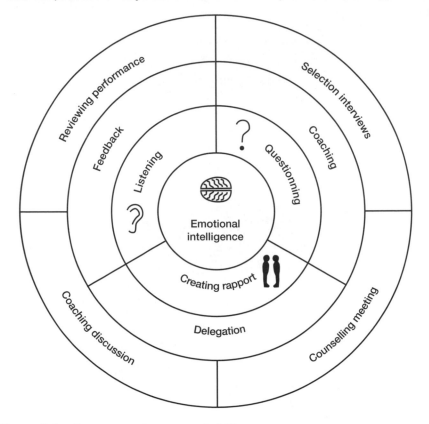

Figure 3.1   Core competences and skills

Assessing your Skills

The importance of emotional intelligence is depicted in Figure 3.1.

The Self-assessment box below will help you to measure your ability in the core competency of emotional intelligence and the key skills of listening, questioning and creating rapport. You can always adapt and use this assessment to ask your team to provide you with feedback. This can be especially useful as often we are not aware of how others see us. Our perception of ourselves can sometimes be very different from the reality that others experience.

Think about each statement and rate yourself accordingly using the four-point scale:

1. Not competent   *Not skilled in this area.*
2. Some competence   *A slight ability demonstrated in this area.*
3. Fairly competent   *An average ability demonstrated in this area.*
4. Very competent   *An above average ability in this area.*

Try to be as honest and objective as possible.

Circle one response for each item on the scale.

Take your time with each item and think about specific examples or situations that demonstrate the competency.

Self-assessment Measuring Emotional Intelligence and Key Skills of Listening, Questioning and Creating Rapport

1	I am receptive to others' ideas and views.	1 2 3 4
2	I ask open questions to encourage a two-way dialogue.	1 2 3 4
3	I adapt my behaviour and management style to different people and situations.	1 2 3 4
4	I understand what motivates others.	1 2 3 4
5	I take time to listen to others.	1 2 3 4
6	I use questions to develop and challenge ideas.	1 2 3 4
7	I develop trust when working with others.	1 2 3 4
8	I recognise my own emotions and their effect on others.	1 2 3 4
9	I give full attention to others when they voice their ideas and concerns.	1 2 3 4
10	I probe for what others really think and check understanding.	1 2 3 4
11	I create rapport and put others at ease.	1 2 3 4
12	I demonstrate honesty and integrity.	1 2 3 4
13	I pick up on others' concerns and issues.	1 2 3 4
14	I use questioning to show an interest in the other person.	1 2 3 4
15	I help others feel at ease.	1 2 3 4
16	I demonstrate emotional resilience in stressful situations.	1 2 3 4

Transfer your scores for each question onto the score sheet below, then add up each column to obtain the total score.

Q	A	Q	B	Q	C	Q	D
1		2		3		4	
5		6		7		8	
9		10		11		12	
13		14		15		16	
Total							

Your A score refers to your listening skills.
Your B score refers to you questioning skills.
Your C score refers to you ability to create rapport.
Your D score refers to your emotional intelligence skills.

If you scored 16 in each section – congratulations, your skills are at a very high level and perfectly honed. Alternatively, you may have been overly generous with your scoring.

If you scored 10 or less in any section you would benefit from developing your skills.

Use this chapter to hone your skills and focus on the development activities provided to help build your confidence and ability.

The Core Competence – Emotional Intelligence

Emotional intelligence is now a commonly used phrase. The concept has been around for centuries but it was Daniel Goleman who demonstrated that it can play a key role in managing relationships and determining leadership success.

Hay group identified four components of emotional intelligence:

1. **Self-awareness** – refers to your ability to understand yourself, to have good self-assessment of yourself and to have self-confidence in how you act.
2. **Self-management** refers to your self-control and adaptability in different situations. It is also linked to your general approach to achievement, goal setting and having an optimistic approach.
3. **Social awareness** is concerned with your ability to show empathy with and understanding of others. This also applies to understanding the organisation and customers.
4. **Relationship management** is your ability to influence others and build relationships and is associated with managing change and conflict.

In looking at these descriptions you can probably identify areas where you are more skilled than others. Don't despair though, the great thing about emotional intelligence is that it can be developed and learnt. It just takes some commitment from you to want to develop and improve your skills.

Tips for Success

Components of Emotional Intelligence	Tips for Development
Self-awareness	1. Gain feedback from others about your approach 2. Monitor your emotions and consider how you come across to others 3. Seek 360° feedback 4. Complete some psychometric questionnaires to understand more about your style and approach 5. Be clear about your personal values and goals

Components of Emotional Intelligence	Tips for Development
Self-management	1. Monitor your emotions and recognise when you use them inappropriately 2. Learn to label your behaviours rather than just randomly expressing them, e.g. 'I'm feeling frustrated with this project', rather than just showing your frustration 3. Take some time for reflection before you speak. 4. Consider the impact of your behaviour on others 5. Create a sense of achievement by setting and monitoring goals
Social awareness	1. Take the time to listen to others 2. Consider feelings alongside other factors when making decisions 3. Work on the skills of developing rapport with others 4. Understand the culture of the organisation and the people you are working with 5. Understand the needs of the different stakeholders you work with

Components of Emotional Intelligence	Tips for Development
Relationship management	1. Plan how to influence people effectively 2. Take a positive approach to managing change 3. Work with your team to build a collaborative environment (see Chapter 7 for tips) 4. Take time to build relationships with your team whether it is face-to-face or over the phone

The skills of listening, questioning and building rapport, covered next, are essential in developing and demonstrating a high level of emotional intelligence and will influence your success in all the component parts of the EI model, so take some time now to master these skills.

The Key Skills – Listening, Questioning and Creating Rapport

The key skills of listening, questioning and creating rapport can help in the preparation and planning for any conversation.

Listening

Listening is at the core of any communication. As well as ensuring a message is really understood, it also gives the talker a sense of self-worth, a feeling that they and their ideas are being heard.

You may be thinking at this stage that you are a good listener, but most of us definitely have room to improve. Look at the questions below:

- Are you often too busy to stop and listen to people?
- Are you often unavailable?
- Do you sometimes try to do two things at once, e.g. answer e-mails and talk on the phone?
- Do you sometimes have other things on your mind when you are listening to someone?
- Do you sometimes try to finish people's sentences?
- Do you often try to cut the conversation short?
- Do you sometimes restrict a conversation to just the part that interests you?
- In meetings do you have side conversations when someone else is talking?
- Do you work in a busy environment where there are lots of distractions?

If you answered 'yes' to any of these questions the chances are that you could benefit from focusing on your listening skills.

The benefits of good listening are enormous. If you are listening well, not only will you be hearing exactly what the person is saying, you will be receiving new ideas and understanding. The other person will have an opportunity to express themselves. This can build their confidence and create greater trust and involvement with you and the team.

This is especially important when you don't have much time with people. One manager with teams spread throughout Europe knows that when a team contacts her, they need her full attention. As such, she makes sure that she clears her mind to give them that focus. '*I need to build trust and I know when they call me, the issue must be important so I give them my full attention.*'

In addition, if you want to influence someone, you really need to listen to their issues and concerns first. All good negotiators spend more time listening and questioning than they do dominating the conversation.

So, half-listening is not enough and the chances are that it may have a negative effect. When you are listening, it is not a just a matter of listening to the words people are saying. It is equally important to pick up on a whole host of others signs which might provide some insight into the feelings, concerns and subtext of the conversation.

Looking for any changes in body language, eye movements, colouration of the skin, or tone and pace of the voice can provide you with some indication that there is something behind the words which may not be immediately evident.

If you are talking to someone over the phone pay special attention to the tone and pace of the conversation. Does the person stumble over their words, rush sentences, change the volume and tone of their voice? These small changes can indicate concerns and worries which may be worth following up on.

It is also important to listen to the specific words someone uses to uncover their commitment and intention. For example, if someone is talking in terms of '*must's*', '*should's*' or '*ought's*', they are not likely to be totally committed to moving ahead. The issues may be causing some stress or pressure. However, if someone is talking about what they '*can*' and '*want*' to do, their intentions and commitment are very clear.

Good listening takes concentration and effort. Here are some tips and techniques to help you enhance your skills.

Tips for success

1. Make sure you have the time and space to listen well. Move away from your work and clear your mind so that you can give the person 100% of your attention.
2. Show that you are interested in what they have to say. That means clear eye contact, leaning forward, nodding and paying attention to them. On the phone, it means listening at three levels to what is being said:
   - Content – language (especially repeated and/or stressed words), pitch, tone, speed
   - Emotion – what feelings is the person experiencing now?

- Intention – what do they need from you? Is it information, reassurance or space to talk things through?
3. Use summarising as a way of checking out your understanding. (It is also a very good way of politely moving the conversation along.)
4. You can also paraphrase the last few words of the sentence, e.g. '*So you're thinking of moving on?*'
5. If you pick up any signals from someone's body language or voice it may be worth checking this out by reflecting back their feelings and asking. '*Is there anything else bothering you?*' or, '*You seem to be a bit worried about x.*'
6. Don't feel you always have to fill the space. Silence in a conversation can help the other person think. You can often tell if the person is reflecting on something if their eyes are either moving or focused elsewhere. When they have finished reflecting they will generally focus on you again.

Next time you have to listen to someone, use the tips above and afterwards, reflect on the conversation to see if you really did put good listening into practice.

Questioning

The second core skill you need to focus on is questioning. Carefully used questions can help to explore ideas in more depth. They also demonstrate that you are listening and paying attention to the other person.

Before you begin a conversation it is important to think about the purpose of the questions you are going to ask. In an interview or selling situation, questions are used to elicit information, whilst in a coaching situation your purpose may be to help the individual to come up with their own solution.

Whatever the scenario, it is always a good idea to plan the questions you want to ask and avoid some of the pitfalls. You need to make sure that the questions work for you and for the person you are talking to.

Table 3.1 Types of questions and when to use them

Type of Question	When to Use It	Examples
Open	■ To establish rapport ■ To gain background information ■ To explore ideas/opinions and attitudes	*Can you tell me about your role?* *What approach do you take?* *What is your opinion on. . .?*
Probing	■ To show interest ■ To dig a bit deeper and explore an issue in more detail. ■ To show understanding.	*What makes you say that?* *I'm really interested in X, can you tell me more?*
Reflective	■ To check understanding. ■ To explore a topic in more depth. ■ To reflect facts and feelings.	*You seem very happy with things?* *So your challenge is managing the team?*
Clarifying	■ To test understanding.	*So what you are saying is. . .?* *Can you just clarify the situation?*
Closed	■ If you want a clear 'yes' or 'no' from the other person. ■ If you want to check a fact.	*Do you know the chief exec of this company?*
Multiple	■ Never: the person will end up answering the last question you asked and this may take you off-track. It is much better to split these down into individual questions.	*What have you enjoyed about your past role, what are you looking forward to and what do think will be the biggest challenge?*
Leading	■ Never: they can distort the conversation.	*We are looking for someone who deals well with customers, how do you rate your skills here?*

Table 3.1   continued

Type of Question	When to Use It	Examples
Rhetorical	■ This may be useful in some teaching situations but generally your aim should be to get the other person to talk and answer the question	*So how do you develop your team? Well there are four things you need to do . . .*
Hypothetical	■ Useful in testing out scenarios and understanding what the other person might do in a certain situation. ■ Can be useful in coaching or interviewing situations.	*What could have happened if you'd challenged this behaviour earlier?*

Table 3.1 lists some of the main types of questions. In general it is always best to work with open, probing, reflective and clarifying questions as these help to develop the conversation. Leading, multiple and rhetorical questions can distort the issue. Closed questions should also be treated with care. While they have their place in getting facts, they can close down a conversation very quickly by turning it into a 'yes' or 'no' dialogue.

Managers often face problems in asking the right questions. The challenge of listening and thinking about the next question at the same time, of building on what the person is saying and keeping the conversation flowing, are common difficulties which can be overcome.

The best way to do this is by planning. As you progress through this chapter you will have the opportunity to plan questions for different one-to-one situations such as coaching, selection interviewing, performance reviews and feedback discussions.

For all of these scenarios some general rules apply. First think about the purpose of the conversation or meeting. This will help to give you a framework for your questions.

Start the conversation with some general, open enquiries. These should be broad-based questions which provide overview and background information.

Typical general questions are:

- *Can you tell me about your experience with X?*
- *What have you enjoyed about working in the team this year?*
- *How would you like to develop your career in the future?*
- *Can you tell me about the situation you are facing?*

However, too many general questions can mean that a conversation moves around but may not tackle the issue at hand. So, you will also need to plan for questions which will gradually dig down to move the conversation in the direction you want to go.

For example, imagine that you want to review a project with a member of your team. You want to discover what went well and what, if anything, could be improved next time. The questioning might proceed something like this:

- *How did the project go?*
- *What were you pleased about?*
- *What do you think we could improve next time?*
- *How might we do that?*
- *That's interesting, can you tell me more?*
- *So what do you think is really feasible?*
- *How could we get started?*
- *Who could help?*
- *What do you think we should do as a first step?*

Going from the general to the specific with a clear purpose in mind is known as the funnel technique. Once you have completed the funnel you can summarise and move on. Often a conversation will have a number of different funnels in it and by planning and even writing down some key questions as part of your preparation you will be more likely to achieve your objectives and help the other person achieve theirs.

Building rapport

Rapport is the cornerstone of good conversation. If you have rapport with someone the chances are that the conversation will flow more easily, decisions will be made and conflict will be avoided.

What is rapport? And how do you know when you've got it?

Often people describe rapport as:

■ Having a connection.
■ Getting on with someone.
■ Having trust.
■ Putting yourself in other people's shoes.
■ Getting along together.

These are all essential aspects of working effectively with others and building up positive relationships.

In some situations we have natural rapport; relaxing with friends, working with people we have a good relationship with, meeting someone with a similar interest and style. In other situations, it is much harder to create a productive atmosphere.

By understanding how to build rapport and applying a few techniques you will have a greater chance of successfully creating a connection with a person.

There are three main elements to rapport:

■ Body language – how to use your body, especially your voice and facial expressions.
■ Energy – how you present your ideas.
■ Content – what you say.

You can always tell if you have rapport with someone as your body language will be in sync and you will be mirroring each other in your behaviour. You will also be talking at the same pace and with the same degree of energy. You may or may not be agreeing on the content. The interesting thing is that if you have rapport on the first two levels you can disagree on the content and the chances are that you will still be having a good discussion rather than an argument.

However, you may be going into situations where you don't have natural and immediate rapport. For example, with new recruits, customers, an irate employee, a boss you don't get on well with, a subordinate you just don't understand, or a team member who is upset about something that has happened to them.

In all these circumstances you have the ability to develop the conversation in a more positive direction. You can't actually change someone's behaviour but you can alter your own and hope that it will impact on the other person.

The first thing you need to do is to try to set the conversation in an environment that is conducive to developing rapport. Think about the venue and the seating arrangements if you are in a position to engineer this part of the meeting.

Check how the other person is sitting or standing: your aim is to initially match the other's behaviour both in terms of body language and pace. This doesn't mean literally copying them but adopting a similar posture and speed. If the other person is someone who talks quickly using lots of hand actions, aim to try to match the delivery by perhaps increasing or decreasing the amount of energy you put into the conversation. As you develop rapport you will notice that the conversation flows more smoothly and you can then alter the pace if you think it's appropriate.

This technique, known as 'matching and pacing', developed from Neuro-Linguistic Programming (NLP). Look at the case study below to see how it works.

Case study

Tom was having difficulties with one of his team members, Joanne. Somehow they just didn't seem to get on. Tom was quite an efficient manager. His desk was always organised and he prided himself on his time management. He was a quick thinker and often got to solutions quickly. Joanne on the other hand was more disorganised. She liked to talk around problems and work in a more reflective manner. She thought her boss was too rushed and impersonal. Joanne performed well in her job but Tom was concerned that their poor working relationship meant that often their meetings were not as positive as they would have liked.

Tom decided to reflect on his own approach and scheduled the next meeting together in the coffee bar, which was more relaxed than his office. He took a step back and rather than rushing to solutions he spent some time listening to Joanne and matching her style and pace. Tom was more relaxed and reflective and did not jump to solutions. Gradually Tom started to summarise and encouraged Joanne to come up with some action points which they could implement.

The meeting may have taken a little longer, but by consciously working to create rapport it meant that they had a more positive conversation and had started to build up a more productive relationship for the future.

Next time you are in a conversation with someone, reflect on whether you have good rapport with them and what, if anything, you need to do to improve it.

Building rapport virtually is harder, but follows the same principles.

■ On the phone, make sure you smile as you pick it up. This may sound strange, but it does actually affect the tone and timbre of your voice, making you sound more relaxed.
■ Make sure you follow the style of the other person. If their preference

is to chat about social things for a while before getting to the point, engage with them. In some cultures this is just good manners, in others mere time-wasting. So a neutral opening like, 'How are things?' is safer than, 'What do you want?'

■ Make sure you both set aside enough time without interruptions and prepare yourself. This doesn't just mean having all the relevant documentation at hand. It also refers to your emotional state. You need to be able to give your time fully to the situation, and this often requires patience if you are working with people from different cultures and with different languages.

■ Summarise on a regular basis and at the end of the conversation review how useful the meeting was.

■ Folllow up the conversation with an email outlining any agreements and actions.

■ If you are communicating via email take time to reflect on your email and Messenger etiquette. The Anglo-Saxon preference in business seems to be direct, even brusque, interchange. This can seem rude in less direct cultures. And of course you won't get told, so you need to reflect on the impact of your style and adapt it accordingly.

Summary

Remember:
■ To hone your EI skills by developing greater self-awareness, especially in terms of how others see you.
■ Take the time to really listen to what others have to say and listen not only to their words but also to their feelings and intentions
■ Use questioning to explore ideas in more depth and to develop others' ideas.
■ Focus on building rapport and developing positive relationships.

Essential Techniques

The three essential techniques of feedback, coaching and delegating are useful in almost any conversation you may have with your team. They can play an important part in helping to motivate and develop them, and build on the core competences and skills already discussed. The frameworks below provide a means of putting the skills into practice.

Whilst all managers are aware that these techniques are important, they often don't get the attention they deserve. Employees are more likely to ask for an external coach than to see their manager as a source of coaching support. It's almost like a vicious circle – you don't display basic EI in your interactions with one of your team, so they withdraw, you begin to get frustrated, they close down more and before you know it, you have a performance issue!

Investing a bit of time and effort in building effective relationships and using these techniques can turn the vicious circle into a more positive and productive situation.

Feedback

Feedback is important. It helps people to understand their strengths and weaknesses. It can help to build self-awareness and confidence and improve our performance – if it's done well. At its worst it can demotivate and discourage.

There are some very clear 'Do's' and 'Don'ts' about feedback. Look at Table 4.1 and think back to the last time you gave feedback to someone. How effective were you?

The theory sounds fairly straightforward yet managers often face difficulties in putting it into action. Sometimes they feel uncertain about how to balance giving a clear message without hurting the other person's feelings. Sometimes they are not sure about how to control their own emotions or the reaction from others. On any of these tricky occasions, it is good to have a basic script to plan for the feedback conversation. This is where SOFA might help (see Table 4.2).

Table 4.1 Do's and don'ts of feedback

Do's	Don'ts
■ Find the right time and place to have the feedback conversation.	■ Say the first thing that comes into your head.
■ Think about what you are going to say.	■ Make generalised statements.
■ Invite them to appraise their performance.	■ Focus on the person and not the performance.
■ Check your intention. Is it to help improve performance?	■ Get angry.
■ Have the individual's interests at heart.	■ Do all the talking. Ask questions.
■ Focus on the specific performance issue.	■ Avoid responsibility by referring to others.
■ Take responsibility for your words, 'The impact on me was … I saw …'	■ Be judgemental.
■ Be clear, direct and concise.	■ Make false threats.
■ Balance negative with positive.	■ Get defensive if your message is not understood.
■ Work on the things that can be changed.	■ Give the feedback without providing any context.
■ Give the feedback as immediately after the event as possible.	■ Leave the individual with no idea of how to improve their performance.
■ Focus on solutions and provide suggestions and alternatives.	■ Just give feedback on what is going wrong.
■ Ask them for ideas.	■ Avoid giving any feedback at all, in order to avoid hassle or conflict.
■ Check that your listener has understood. Ask them to summarise.	
■ End on a positive note by offering support and reassurance.	
■ Develop a plan together to improve the situation and agree any follow-up.	

Table 4.2 The SOFA model

S	**Situation**	Describe the situation by providing some context and talk specifically about the behaviours which are causing concern.
O	**Outcomes**	Describe the consequences of the behaviour. How does it impact on you and others?
F	**Feelings**	Describe how it makes you feel. This has a number of advantages in that it labels how you feel in a calm way, and describes the impact of the behaviour on you which cannot be disputed.
A	**Action**	It is always important to agree some actions and a way forward. This may be in terms of coaching, setting improvement objectives and agreeing a time to follow up and review the changes.

SOFA is a model which will help you explain the position, describe the outcomes of the behaviour and allow you to express your feelings about the matter. It then moves into identifying what can be done to rectify and improve the situation.

Case study

John is always very vocal in meetings and often criticises other people's ideas without exploring them fully. At the last team meeting when one of the junior members (Peter) suggested ways of sharing information and ideas across the group, John came up with a string of reasons why this would not work, leaving Peter feeling deflated and patronised.

While some of John's ideas were valid you are concerned that his style and approach is coming across as bullying and is resulting in reduced input and ideas from other team members.

Using the SOFA technique and referring to the 'Do's' and 'Don'ts' of feedback, think about how to provide some constructive feed-back for John.

Think about:

■ The specific behaviour you want to draw to John's attention.
■ The effect on others.
■ The effect on you.
■ How you could develop a way forward together.

How about this?

John, I want to talk to you about the recent meeting we had. I always welcome your ideas and involvement, but in this case I was concerned that when Peter suggested some new ways of working you came in very forcefully with a list of reasons why his idea wouldn't work. The outcome was that Peter didn't contribute any further to the meeting. I know that some of your comments were valid but it left me feeling very concerned about the impact of your behaviour. I'd like us to look at how you keep up your input and involvement in the meeting but in a way that encourages others to join in the debate.

Obviously a live conversation would be two-way and John may become defensive. This reaction can lead to conflict so here are a few tips to keep the feedback on-line.

Tips for Success

■ Listen to what the person has to say (they may have some valid comments).
■ Don't be afraid of any silences in the conversation. It is a useful way of helping the other person think through the issue.
■ Don't get drawn into arguments. If possible, refer to the positives about the person. In John's case this could be: 'I really welcome

> *your inputs and feel that they would be even more valuable if they were delivered in a more positive way.'*
>
> ■ Try to use 'Yes, and' rather than 'Yes, but' as in the sentence above. People are often waiting for the latter which can appear negative rather than the former which is more positive and constructive.
>
> ■ Give some clear reasons for changing the behaviour. Identify the benefits to the individual and others.
>
> ■ If there are any consequences of not changing, these may need to be voiced.
>
> ■ Remain calm and focused and don't get drawn into using emotive language.
>
> ■ If you reach an impasse, ask the person to think about the feedback and arrange a meeting to discuss it further.

Once the feedback has been discussed and accepted, you may need to help the individual identify what they need to do next. This may involve some coaching and support to help them rectify the situation.

However, beware. When people receive difficult feedback they can go into a shock cycle where they struggle to accept and make sense of the comments. They may not be able to listen to anything you are saying because they launch into the SARA cycle.

The first stage is literally
shock (S) followed by
anger (A) then
rejection (R) and finally
acceptance (A). One manager I spoke to told me about a time he received a poor appraisal rating. He just sat there and couldn't remember the rest of the conversation. The message here is that it's always important to check out how people are feeling after receiving feedback and sometimes arrange another meeting when they have come to terms with it and are ready to move on.

If you ever find yourself in this situation try not to become defensive. This is easier said than done, but here are a few tips to help you through the SARA cycle:

Tips for Success

- Listen to what is being said. It's an opportunity to learn about yourself
- Be sure you understand precisely what is being said. You may want to summarise or paraphrase what has been said
- Rather than becoming defensive it is always better to ask questions to explore the feedback such as, 'Can you give me a specific example?' or 'What makes you think that ...?'
- Share your reactions to what has been said so that the other person knows what you are thinking and feeling.
- If you are not sure of exactly what has been raised, check out the feedback with others.
- If you want time to let the feedback sink in, ask for another meeting.
- Try to look for ways forward. How can you change the situation for the future?
- Remember that is often difficult for the other person, so try to understand their perspective and thank them for the feedback.
- Finally, you need to decide what you want to do. Take some time to think and reflect. Don't overreact and when you are ready, work on a plan for the future.

However, remember that feedback shouldn't just focus on the negatives. Chapter 1 describes how positive feedback and praise is an important factor in delivering improved performance. If people know they are doing something well, the likelihood is that they will do more of it.

We often fall into the trap of forgetting the positive feedback or generalising it, saying things like, 'That was great', 'You did really well in that presentation' or, 'The client was impressed with your work.' Whilst they are positive statements, it would be more beneficial to the individual to find out specifically what it was they did well in the presentation, or specifically what the client liked so that it can be replicated in the future. So, remember to use the SOFA approach in all feedback situations, not just the difficult ones.

Coaching

Coaching has entered the management world and is becoming more and more popular. It is one of the key management skills you can build into everyday conversations to help people to grow and develop. As a tool it can help you to lead and delegate more effectively, and ensure that feedback is translated into new behaviours and skills for the future. In addition, it can be used to find fresh and creative solutions to difficult problems, helping both the individual and the team move forwards.

So what is coaching? It's about:

■ Helping someone find their own solution.
■ Bringing out the creativity in others.
■ Unlocking potential.
■ Stepping back and letting the other person take responsibility for their learning.
■ Turning problems into learning opportunities.

It is not about overdirecting, teaching, or taking over responsibility.

To become a good coach, you need to work on the key skills of listening, questioning and rapport building. You also need a '*coaching mindset*'; a set of beliefs about your role and about the people you are coaching.

These beliefs are very important in developing the right attitude and approach. Developing a coaching mindset means you believe that:

■ Other people have the resources to move the issue forward.
■ There are lots of different ways to approach and solve the issue at hand.
■ Other people have creative ideas.
■ You can develop a solution together.
■ In most situations, asking questions to help people explore their thinking is better than telling people what to do.
■ Your role is to help the other person come up with their own solution.

Often, if managers don't have this mindset when they go into a coaching situation they can end up telling people what to do, or asking too many closed or leading questions when more open, exploratory questions would be better.

In general it is always better to ask more open questions, but there may be times when people just need some information and a direct 'Yes' or 'No' answer. But remember that in a good coaching session, it will be the other person who does most of the thinking and comes up with most of the ideas. Not only does this have the potential of generating an even better solution, but it is likely that the individual will be far more committed to achieving the result, as they have a greater understanding of what to do.

It is often useful to have a framework to help guide the coaching conversation. The TOPIC model, Table 4.3, can help you to plan and structure the next coaching conversation you have.

Table 4.3 The TOPIC model

Topic	Identifying the issue to focus on.
Outcomes	Understanding the preferred outcome.
Present situation	Exploring the present situation.
Ideas	Generating ideas to move forward.
Conclusion	Agreeing the next steps and developing an action plan.

The success of the model lies in using good quality, open questions ('killer questions', Table 4.4) which can help to direct the conversation and stimulate the other person's thinking. Their purpose is to help the individual to think more deeply about the issue and any possible solutions.

Table 4.4 Killer questions

TOPIC	What to do	Killer Questions
Topic	This is a very important stage as sometimes the presented issue may not be the real problem. For example, if someone says they want a better work-life balance it will be important to explore what they mean. Is it more time with family, less travelling, a better level of fitness or just less work?	■ What would you like to discuss? ■ Is there any specific aspect you would like to focus on? ■ What is really important to you right now? ■ So what you really want to focus on is …?
Outcome	Setting the outcome is important as it sets some parameters to the issue and helps you both gain a common understanding of what is achievable and acceptable.	■ What do you want to achieve? ■ What will it be like when you get there? ■ What is acceptable for you? ■ Do you have a time scale for achieving this? ■ How will you measure your success?
Present situation	Exploring the present situation can throw some light on what has already been achieved and what needs to happen to move forward.	■ What have you done so far? ■ Have you ever tackled anything like this in the past? ■ Is there anyone who can help you? ■ Is there anyone who you can learn from? ■ What can help you to move ahead?

Table 4.4   continued

TOPIC	What to do	Killer Questions
Ideas	Coming up with ideas to move the situation ahead is a creative process. Often people have more ideas than they originally thought. At this stage you can offer suggestions but do so at the end, and offer them in a tentative way with their permission.	■ So what could you do to achieve your outcome? ■ What else could you do? (It is worth asking this question a number of times, even when they think they have come up with all the possible answers.)
Conclusion	This is where you help the person to identify the next step and set up an action plan. It is always a good thing here to test their commitment to moving ahead. If they aren't committed it may be better to focus on something else. Often, coaching takes time and may take another couple of follow-up meetings to move the situation along.	■ So what will you do as a first step? ■ On a scale of 1 to 10 how committed are you to moving ahead? ■ How will you measure your success? ■ What else will you need to do to move forward?

This framework can be used in all sorts of situations. A coaching session may not always involve separate meetings. Try to incorporate these ideas into your everyday conversations as a way of constantly developing your people.

You may notice that all the questions suggested have a positive slant. They are looking at what can be done to develop and move ahead and what has been achieved. This is very important in coaching as they help to create possibilities and new options.

Case study

One of Sarah's team members, Paul, came into the office very concerned about how things were going with one of his clients. Paul was worried that he was going to lose the contract and wanted Sarah to intervene and sort things out.

Sarah was very tempted to go to the rescue. She needed this order for her own targets and had some knowledge of the client from a previous contract. Yet, instead of reacting and taking the problem on, she questioned Paul about the current situation; what he wanted to achieve. They then explored all the possible ideas which they could focus on to bring the client back on track. Once Paul had calmed down he had quite a few ideas and felt reassured that something could be done. Sarah did offer some ideas from her own experience of working with the client and between them they came up with an action plan which Paul implemented. They also agreed to meet up in a few days' time to discuss progress.

This one example illustrates the power of coaching. Paul was able to identify a way forward and felt confident that he was doing the right thing and Sarah had avoided taking the problem on. She had also helped her team member manage the situation. Sarah felt confident that everything was being done to rectify the issue.

Compare the questions in Table 4.5. Imagine the effect each set would have on you.

Table 4.5 Problem-focused and solution-focused questions

A	B
So what is the problem you face?	What outcome do you want?
How long has it been going on?	What can you do to achieve the
What are the specifics of the	outcome?
problem?	Who can help?
Who is to blame?	What can you do as a next step?
What should you have done?	

The questions in section A have a 'real problem' focus and dig deeper and deeper, eventually lead to blaming, scapegoating and generally being stuck. The questions in section B are framed in a more positive, solution-focused way. They don't avoid the difficulties and challenges but look in a more helpful way at how to overcome them

Next time you are in one of these conversations, reflect on the type of questions you are using as they will have an impact on the motivation and actions of the person you are coaching.

Make time to coach your people, and every time you are tempted to offer a solution, stop for a minute and reflect on whether a good coaching question might be the better option.

Delegating

Coaching and delegating often go hand-in-hand, especially if you are trying to develop the skills and abilities of the person you are delegating to. It is commonly an area where managers face some real challenges.

Managers find it hard to delegate for a number reasons. Look at the list of excuses below :

- I'm too busy to delegate.
- No one can do it as well as I can.

- This is too important.
- I don't have time to explain.
- What will happen to my job if I delegate everything?
- Everyone else is busy too.
- My team don't have the skills.

These issues are often a reflection of the way managers work. Being busy creates a vicious cycle. You don't have time to think about what to delegate and who to delegate to until it is too late so you have to do it yourself. You don't have time to set up the necessary coaching and skills development, so end up late in the office to complete the job. These are very common issues and in addition you may secretly not want to delegate the work … perhaps you enjoy what you do or feel insecure about handing it over.

Self-assessment Looking at Yourself and How You Operate

One way of doing this is to draw a mind map of your job (this technique was used earlier in Chapter 1). Put yourself in the centre and add your key tasks and activities.

When you have done this reflect on the following:

- How much time do you spend on the different parts of your job? Is this what you should be doing or do you get bogged down in other activities? Often managers find that they spend more time on the day-to-day activities and leave little time for the real leadership jobs such as planning, strategic thinking and coaching their people.
- Which parts of your job do you enjoy most and which least? It is often harder to let go of the enjoyable parts of the job, even though they might be better delegated to someone else.
- Which parts of your job could you delegate to others? How would this help your role and how would it help others? What development would you need to put into place to ensure that your people are skilled enough to take these tasks on?
- What new projects and tasks are coming up in the future? Are any of these suitable to delegate to your team?

Once you have taken a good look at yourself and your role, and reflected on what you can delegate, the next stage is to think about your team. In Chapter 1 you had the opportunity to explore what motivates your different team members and reflect on their strengths and weakness. It would be useful to refer to this when thinking about who to delegate work to, in order to match the task to the individual.

For example, one of your team may be more motivated by a task that involves them in presenting and meeting other people whereas another team member may be more interested in a detailed data analysis role.

Figure 4.1 may help you to think about planning your delegation. Which tasks can be used to help to develop your people as well as getting the job done? Using this model also means that you can consider the mix of what you are delegating to people. This will ensure that you are delegating a range of tasks, mixing some of the more boring items with others that provide challenge and learning.

Once you have identified what you want to delegate and who you want to delegate to, the next challenge is how to delegate effectively. Often this is where problems occur so here are a few tips.

	Unimportant	Important
High	Long-term projects Planned development and delegation	Delegation and development Challenges which require coaching Learning new skills
Low	Shifting boring tasks	Most delegation!

Learning

Task

Figure 4.1 The delegation mix

Tips for Success

- Agree what you are delegating in terms of results. Ask the individual to summarise what they intend to do so that you can be sure you have a common understanding.
- Try to delegate the entire task.
- Discuss how they envisage doing the task and encourage them to come up with ideas and take responsibility. Recognise that they will not do it in exactly the same way that you would. They might even do it better!
- Agree times when you will meet up to discuss progress. This is much better than constantly worrying and checking, or leaving it until the end and not being happy with the results.
- Make sure you provide them with the authority to do the task, i.e. give them access to the people and information they may need.
- If they do need coaching and development to achieve the goal make sure it is provided.
- Make sure you give the individual full and public recognition for what they have done as this is often the best reward you can give them.

To put these skills to use you might want to use Table 4.6. It will help you to think about your team, assess their strengths and development needs, and devise an action plan in terms of coaching, delegating and providing feedback.

Table 4.6 Delegation planning

Team Member	Strengths	Development Areas	Coaching, Delegation and Feedback Plan	Date for Completion

Summary

Remember:

- Recognise the power of feedback as a tool to help develop performance in others.
- For tricky feedback situations use the SOFA technique as a way of preparing for what you might say.
- Coaching is an essential management tool and is something you can build into your everyday conversations.
- Coaching and delegation go hand-in-hand. Effective delegation can help you to develop your people and provide you with the opportunity to enhance your own role in the organisation.

Productive
Conversations

The skills tool kit is almost complete. The final challenge is to fit the skills and techniques into a framework for some of the conversations you may get involved in. The first priority with any conversation is planning and preparation. Like many managers, you may be guilty of rushing into a meeting or picking up the phone without thinking about the people involved. Beware; it is in these situations that conversations can go disastrously wrong and misunderstandings occur. Just planning for the logistics of the meeting is not enough. Your success will rest on being clear about the outcome you want in terms of both the task (what needs to happen), the process (how it will happen), and the relationship with the individuals involved.

This chapter focuses on a number of typical conversations and provides frameworks, tips, ideas, and some 'killer questions' to help you put the skills tool kit to best possible use.

Performance Reviews

Performance reviews are an important part of working with others in your team, so the first point is DON'T put them off. Make sure that you set up regular times throughout the year to review performance with each individual. The real success of any performance management system rests on the quality of the conversation between an individual and their manager. A review provides a fantastic opportunity to spend time with your team to consider their performance and plan ahead.

The tips and reminders below will illustrate how you can make this conversation a productive one for all concerned.

Before the Review

- Make sure you have booked a private room and allowed sufficient time free from interruptions.

- Both you and the appraisee need time to prepare so that you are both clear about what you want to get out of the meeting.
- Collect feedback from other people. (This is especially important if the person you are appraising has been working in a different location or across a number of projects.)
- Think about the feedback you want to give the individual. What have they done well, and what could they improve on?
- Plan the structure for the meeting and think about any questions you may want to ask.

During the Review

- Spend some time building rapport and outlining the structure of the meeting.
- Make sure you spend time reviewing performance as well as planning for the coming year.
- Make sure you do more listening than talking, and use your questioning skills to probe and develop any ideas that emerge.
- Provide constructive feedback and focus on what you appreciate about the individual's performance before looking at the areas for improvement.
- Make sure you keep the meeting on track by regularly summarising where you are, and where the discussion needs to go.
- Develop a plan for the future with clear, agreed objectives and ensure that you also have time to discuss development and training needs which can help the individual perform better.

After the Review

- Make sure that all actions, objectives and plans are recorded. (Often the appraisee is in the best position to do this, and it means that you can ensure that you have joint agreement on the outcome of the meeting.)
- Set up a date for a review meeting. Ideally this should be on a quarterly basis so that you can both review and monitor progress.

Here are a few killer questions that will help.

- What have been the highlights of your achievements this year?
- What aspects of your work have not gone as well? Why?
- Looking at the competences for your role, how well do feel you have met them?
- What do think are your strengths? How are they being used? How could we build on them?
- What do you think are your weaker areas? How could we improve them?
- How do you want to develop in the longer term? What sort of training or development do you need to get there?
- What can I do more of to help you succeed in your role?

Selection Interviews

If you are in the position to recruit a new team member you need to make sure you have done everything you can to select the right person for the job. Recruitment mistakes are costly and you often have to live with them for a very long time, so don't cut any corners.

Usually, as a line manager, your involvement in selection may be in terms of internal recruitment, or in assisting with external recruitment. In the latter case, your HR department will generally have devised the recruitment process from the initial stages of developing the job description and personal specification, and placing advertisements, right through to sifting through the CV's, devising the interview process (which may have included psychometric questionnaires, exercises and group work as well as interviews) and, in the final agreement, terms and conditions. You will need to work with them to ensure that your specific requirements are being met and that together you can really select the best person for the role.

Below are some key areas for you to focus on before, during and after the selection process.

Before the Interview

- Draw up an accurate Job Description – this should outline the purpose and scope of the role, the reporting lines, key responsibilities, and any performance measures and deliverables.
- In addition you will need to have a clear person specification, outlining the qualifications required, the intellectual demands of the job, the skills and competences required, personal attributes and motivation.
- These features can be used to draw up any advertising material and also to assess and short list any applications and CV's. The chart below can be adapted for the different roles you may be recruiting for.
- You will also need to devise some very specific questions which can be used to assess the individual's potential and capabilities.
- If you are interviewing with someone else, or taking part in a panel interview, ensure that you have time to meet with your colleagues to plan how you are going to work together and what specific areas you will be responsible for.

Table 5.1 can be used to help you develop your interview plan and devise appropriate questions.

Table 5.1 Interview plan

Candidate's Name			Interviewer		
Criteria	Sources of Information				Explore – Questions
	CV	Education	Experience	Interests/ Hobbies	
Intellectual demands of the job					
Skills with people					
Results/Achievements					
Personal attributes					
Motivation					
Managerial experience					

Planning the right questions

Devising questions which assess the capabilities of the individual and verify any information is important. You will also need to probe deeply to look for clear evidence and to identify something about the motivation and values which drive the individual to achieve (see Table 5.2).

The preparation you do at this stage will reap distinct benefits as it will help you to be more focused in the interview and be clear about the type of person you require for the role.

Table 5.2 Specific questions for identifying competences and behaviours

Influence	Describe a situation where you had to persuade someone to do something which they didn't want to do. What approach did you take? Was this approach appropriate?
Working with people	Can you tell me about a time when you worked closely within a group or team where there was a conflict? What effect did this have on you and other members of the group? How did you cope?
Communication	Can you tell me about a situation when you found it difficult to communicate with an individual or a group of people? What do you think made the communication difficult? What did you do?
Planning	Could you describe a time when you had to plan a major project and oversee its completion? How closely did the project conform to your plans? What did you do when the project appeared to be slipping?

Table 5.2   continued

Analytical	Can you describe a time when you had to choose between short-term returns and long-term benefits? What influenced your choice?
Decision making	Could you tell me about a time when you had to make a business decision which affected others. How did you make the decision?
Self-motivation	How have your career goals changed over the past two years?
Innovation	What has been the best idea you have come up with to make a job easier?
Sales and marketing	Can you tell me about a situation when you met or exceeded a customer's service expectations? How did you identify what was most important to the customer in this situation?

During the Interview

The interview process has three main phases:

1. Welcoming the individual and putting them at ease.
2. Exploring and acquiring information about the candidate.
3. Supplying information about the company and closing the interview.

1. Welcome
   - Remember the candidate will probably be nervous so spend time building rapport and putting them at ease.
   - Explain the process and timing. Remember it is a two-way decision – the candidate will also be deciding whether they want to work for you!
   - Start with some general exploratory questions to find out a little about the individual.

2. Exploring and acquiring information
   - This is where your preparation will be rewarded. Use the funnel technique to delve into specific areas and competences (see p. 69).
   - Listen to facts, feeling and values so that you can really assess the individual's key strengths.
   - Probe, using the questions you prepared beforehand, to establish key facts and patterns of behaviour.
   - Remember that the candidate should be doing most of the talking so make sure your questions are good open questions.

3. Supplying information
   - This is an important part of helping the candidate understand more about the role and the organisation, so make sure you can provide sufficient background in this area. Often the HR department play a valuable role here in talking through benefits and terms and conditions.
   - Allow time for the candidate to ask questions.
   - Explain what happens next and thank them for coming for the interview.

Evaluation and follow-up

Whilst the interview is important, it needs to be evaluated alongside all the other information you may have about the candidate. This may include psychometric questionnaires, feedback from group exercises, references and feedback from other managers, etc. It is only when you are in a position to make a clear, informed decision that you should make your final choice.

You will also need to provide feedback to candidates who are not successful. This is particularly important with internal recruitment decisions as it is vital to keep the individual motivated. Feedback from the interview can be added to any development planning for the future.

Coaching Interviews

The skills of coaching were covered in Chapter 4, and whilst you have been encouraged to build them into your day-to-day conversations, you may want to set up a specific coaching meeting to assist one of your team in developing their skills and abilities in some way. The list below provides structure for this process.

1. Agree the development need.
2. Identify a suitable project.
3. Agree the task and outcomes.
4. Use the TOPIC model to generate ideas and actions.
5. Identify and agree a process of follow-up and review.
6. Monitor progress and review the result.

The following case study illustrates how useful a specific coaching meeting can be.

Case study

Jane recognised that one of her team members, Richard, needed to build up his confidence and communication skills before he could be considered for promotion. Richard was very capable but didn't have much visibility in the team. This had been recognised as a development need in his recent appraisal. Jane set up a meeting with the specific purpose of looking at this issue. She knew that in the next month she would need to prepare and give a presentation to the senior management team. Jane suggested that this might be a suitable project for Richard to help with. He could present some of the projects the team had been working on. Richard agreed to this idea and they spent the meeting looking at what preparation was required and, using the TOPIC model, they came up with a list of actions and design ideas for the presentation. Richard agreed to prepare some of the material and they both decided on a follow-up day to review the material and practice the presentation together. This would provide a second coaching opportunity and give Richard the support and development he needed to complete the final presentation.

The result was that Richard made a successful presentation and developed the confidence to represent the team in other meetings. Jane also benefited in that she was able to delegate more of this work to Richard, which then gave her the opportunity to focus on more strategic issues.

As you can see from this example the time spent coaching can reap rewards in terms of a better trained and more confident team. You can also pass on your coaching skills so that you create a coaching culture in the team where more experienced people teach and develop the newer members.

Counselling Discussions

From time to time individuals in your team will need some support and counselling. Your role is an important one here, in helping to work through the issue and refer them to appropriate support networks.

It is important to remember that as a manager you are not a trained counsellor, so it would be unfair to expect you to have the experience and skills of a professional.

However, there are some things you can do to help the individual and yourself in this situation and the tips below provide some ideas.

Tips for Success

1. Your role is very much a listening one, so make sure you give your full attention and just listen. You will need to listen at the level of *facts, feelings* and *intentions*.
2. Using reflective questions can help to show you are listening and encourage the other person to talk. Try not to offer solutions but use coaching questions to help them think through the next steps.
3. Create good rapport – this will mean matching the individual's body language. For example, if they are leaning forward, you do the same and then gradually sit up and move into a more a positive position. The chances are that the individual will match your style and once they are in a more positive position, the likelihood is that they will start to feel a little more positive.
4. You will need to set some parameters for the meeting and be clear about what you can do, and where your skills and responsibilities end. In addition issues of confidentiality need to be discussed.
5. Setting up support mechanisms is important. Often the HR department can help to provide ongoing counselling support or refer the individual to a professional organisation.
6. Remember that your colleague may be going through the SARA cycle (see p. 80) and may want to express themselves emotionally. All you can do is provide support at this stage and recognise that they may need time and space to move on.
7. Agree a follow-up and any specific actions. Don't expect to solve the issue in just one meeting.
8. Finally, recognise that often *you* need support when you are dealing with difficult situations. Professional counsellors will always have supervision so it may be worth finding a bit of coaching support for yourself. If you are feeling out of your depth make sure that you refer the individual to someone who has more experience in this area.

Summary

Your skills in working with others on a one-to-one basis are vital and can help you manage a whole range of one-to-one conversations.

Remember:

- Preparation is the key to success in any one-to-one conversation.
- A successful performance review can help to motivate and inspire your team to improve their performance.
- Spending time preparing for a selection interview can avoid a lot of costly and often irreversible mistakes.
- Time spent coaching and counselling your people will pay dividends in terms of business results and overall performance.

Other one-to-one situations such as managing conflict, managing upwards and influencing effectively will be explored in Chapters 7 and 8.

3

Building High-Performing Teams

Building High-Performing Teams

One-to-one relationships are the essential building blocks for successful teams, but there are additional issues in getting groups to function well and become effective teams. Once you have more than one person to manage, you have a whole new set of interpersonal dynamics.

The complexity and nature of team work creates its own challenges. Working in a global environment means that virtual and cross-cultural working is more prevalent. In addition, cross-functional and short-term project teams are needed to provide flexible responses to our changing competitive environment.

This section examines the challenges of working in today's team environment and provides you with the tools and techniques to build a sustainable high-performing team despite the challenges you may face.

6

Analysing Your Team

The first thing to consider is the depressing fact that a large number of teams fail to achieve their goals, with considerable cost to the organisation and the people involved. The five most commonly cited reasons are outlined below. Do you recognise any of them in teams you have worked in?

1. The Task Governs the Process

Whilst the task is the central focus and purpose of the team, there is much more to achieving success than this. Working as a team requires that you pay attention to relationships and the way you work and communicate. Teams need to find ways to build trust, to understand the strengths and weaknesses of each member and to gain a sense of commitment to the overall goal. If you want your team to go the extra mile you will need to understand them as individuals and help to create an environment where they can work creatively together. Focusing purely on the task without addressing team dynamics can lead to failure.

If this is affecting your team go to Chapter 7 and explore the many ways you can build the focus and commitment to achieve the task and maintain the motivation they need.

2. Forgetting About the Stakeholders

A stakeholder is anyone who has an influence on, or interest in, the team. They may be a sponsor, senior manager, team member boss, manager of a different department, client or customer. Each and every one of these people can have a positive or negative influence on the team's outcome. They can create visibility and support for the group, help to provide access to people and resources and emphasise the importance of the team's work. The world of influence and organisational politics is not one which can be ignored.

If stakeholder support is affecting the success of your team use the action lists and tips provided in Chapter 8 to help you to manage upwards and outwards with greater effect.

3. Unclear Expectations

Expectations are vitally important. The team need to know what and when they are to deliver and the stakeholders should have the same understanding. If outcomes are not clear and negotiated with all parties, you may be expected to deliver the impossible. It is important not only to be clear about these, but also to agree the performance around the team and the individuals. If the team don't know what is expected or 'how' they work together – their contribution, time commitment, performance and quality levels – they are unlikely to work in unison.

At an individual level, team members will have expectations about what sort of leadership they require. They may have their own development and preferences in mind and specific ways of working which need to be taken into account.

Case study

Frank was a troubleshooter working for a large engineering company. He had a temporary team, brought together to look at the operations processes in the department with a view to recommending more efficient ways of working. The team of five engineers represented different parts of the production cycle. Initially the team struggled. Some members seemed uncommitted, arriving late for meetings and showing little enthusiasm. It was only when Frank talked to the team that he realised they were also trying to work on other projects and couldn't see what was 'in it for them' to contribute to this project. Realising the problem, Frank worked with the team to set up some clear expectations around the scope of the project and the time required. He also discussed individual expectations – people's work preferences, learning goals and aspirations – and looked at how the project could be used to fulfil these needs. In addition, he agreed to provide feedback for all team members which would become part of the company's appraisal and reward scheme. Agreeing and sharing team and individual expectations meant that everyone was clear about their contribution. This in turn helped to build motivation and commitment.

Without clear expectations at both a team and an individual level, motivation and commitment will fall away.

If your team has unclear expectations focus on the Purpose and Performance sections in Chapter 7.

4. Ignoring Interpersonal and Team Issues

The interpersonal issues, conflict management, creativity and sense of fun and satisfaction team members get from working together is an important factor of performance management that is often ignored. If it is, the team can frequently develop unproductive ways of working. Conflict can escalate, team members lose motivation and commitment, cooperation diminishes and creativity vanishes. Teams develop patterns of working together and some of these patterns can be counterproductive.

Case study

Rachael managed a team of graphic designers in an advertising agency. She noticed that two new group members did not contribute much and over a period of weeks, it became the norm that their opinion was neither sought nor respected. Rachael needed to break the cycle by bringing the designers into the meeting and making sure their views were heard. The team were surprised by the creativity and insight these quiet members brought into the discussion.

If communication and conflict are issues, refer to the Relationships and Communication section in Chapter 7.

5. Team Leadership

Leadership can take many forms. The most important thing is that there *is* leadership. Leadership needs to be developed as the team grows in confidence and moves through the various stages of its evolution. Different styles are suited to different stages. Teams where there is no leadership or the wrong sort rarely succeed. If you are always leading from the front, beware that the team will let you, at a cost to their development and your stress levels. However, a lack of leadership will lead to all the problems associated with unclear expectations and standards. Getting the balance right and developing the skills to pass on leadership to the team is essential if you want to achieve a goal where everyone is committed and involved.

> **Case study**
>
> *Helen came into an accounts department that was failing badly. Procedures were non-existent and paperwork processes inconsistent. At first, Helen was directive in establishing the checks and systems she felt were necessary for the department to deliver. However, once these were in place she felt she could take a more consultative role, working with the team to help them to develop the processes further.*

If you want to reflect on your leadership approach use the questionnaires and models in Chapter 8 to understand the impact you may be having on your team.

The list above represents just a few of the most common reasons for team failure. The consequences of ignoring these issues can be disastrous. It is also worth remembering that the more complex the team, the greater the chance of team failure. Research shows that less than 30% of virtual teams are seen to be effective and successful. Team development is not a 'nice to have', it is a prerequisite for success.

Given that the type and complexity of your team will have an impact on the potential for success, it is worth spending some time analysing the type of group you are working with, and then identifying the appropriate strategies for building performance.

The first stage is to find out whether you really are working as a team, or whether you are just a group of people who are working together independently. If that's the case there is little point in spending the time and effort in building a team. For example, a group of financial analysts focusing on different markets and different products may not be operating as a team. Their roles are completely independent and they will be individually accountable for what they do. As their manager focus instead on individual issues and help everyone achieve their specific objectives.

Teams are usually defined by the fact that they have a common goal. They should rely on each other to achieve the task, be mutually accountable and have the ability to learn and grow together. In this case your role should definitely be to develop the team, realising the synergies between the individual members

What Type of Team are You?

Once you have decided that you are a team, the next stage is to reflect on what type of team you are. There are many different types of teams in operation and each type of team will need a slightly different focus

Steady State or *Ad Hoc* Team

Steady state team

Steady state teams are those that have been working together over a long period, whilst *ad hoc* teams are usually brought together for a specific purpose. If you are leading the former your challenge will be to develop and maintain a motivated, high-performing team, which can integrate new members and adapt to new challenges and objectives.

Table 6.1 Advantages and disadvantages of steady state teams

Advantages	Possible Problem Areas
■ The team has been through the initial processes and is stable. ■ Team members know each other well. ■ Everyone is aware of their role. ■ If working well together the team will be able to support each other and adapt to new changes and ideas.	■ The team may have become fixed in their ways, perhaps a little stale. ■ There may be friction amongst some team members and it may be difficult to integrate new members. ■ The team may become complacent. ■ They may lack the creativity or drive to respond to change.

The advantages and disadvantages of steady state teams are shown in Table 6.1.

Ad hoc teams

The advantages and disadvantages of *ad hoc* teams are shown in Table 6.2.

Table 6.2 Advantages and disadvantages of *ad hoc* teams

Advantages	Possible Problem Areas
■ There is a clean slate to work with. ■ The team probably has a clear purpose. ■ Team members will bring a diversity of skills and approaches. ■ If everyone is focused on the objective these teams can provide a creative, dynamic response to change.	■ 'Short-termism' may be an issue. ■ Ensuring that the goal and purpose is clear and agreed. ■ Providing the time for team members to develop trust and understand each other's roles and contribution. ■ Team members may have conflicting demands from elsewhere in the business.

For *ad hoc* teams, your challenge will be to accelerate the development of the team so that members can work together effectively and maintain a focus on their overall objective.

Team Size

If your team is less than four you may need to bring in other people from time to time to help to generate ideas. If your team in bigger than eight, you may need to break it into smaller sub-teams. Once above twelve, your team may be quite unwieldy. This can often create inefficiencies in managing meetings, communicating effectively, and structuring, so you will need to look at the possibility of setting up sub-teams and considering other ways of passing on information.

What Development Stage is Your Team At?

It is also important to think about what stage of development your team has reached. In 1965, Tuckman suggested that teams move through a number of stages: *forming, storming, norming,* and *performing.* The *forming* stage happens when a new team comes together or when new members enter the team. At this stage the team get to know each other, to understand each other's perspective, and agree a common purpose and goal. Next, teams will generally go through a *storming* phase where conflicts, misunderstandings and personality issues come to the surface. These need to be dealt with for the team to move on. After this the development phase involves agreeing some ground rules, some *norms,* and ways they can work together. Once norms are established, the team can use this platform to move into a high-*performing* phase, working creatively together and having fun.

Tuckman later added another important stage, that of *adjourning,* when the task is complete or the team moves on. This stage is often forgotten, but the chance to review and capitalise on team learning, provide feed-

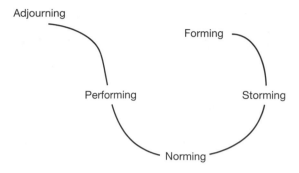

Figure 6.1 Stages of team development

back to each other and reflect on the achievement with key stakeholders is vitally important.

Team life, of course, is far more complex than this. New members, changing goalposts and conflicting demands and priorities mean that teams may be moving backwards and forwards around the various stages. The real secret of team leadership is to understand what stage your team is at, and work to accelerate its development so that you can move as quickly as possible to become a high-performing unit. Table 6.3 is a checklist to help you identify the stage your team is at, and some of the interventions and approaches you could take. The next chapter will focus on the tools and techniques which can move your team through the cycle and develop their performance.

Just how Complex is Your Team?

Teams vary in the complexity of their make-up and structure. With the growth in home working and the increase in global business, teams are becoming more dispersed, spread across countries, cultures and time zones. This can have a dramatic influence on the way the team works. Communication, cultural differences and trust building are typical of the team dynamics which require particular attention to avoid conflict and misunderstandings.

Table 6.3 Team stage, interventions and approaches

Stages	Possible Issues	Suggested Approaches
Forming	■ Getting to know each other ■ Developing a shared purpose and goal. Understanding the stakeholder needs ■ Gaining commitment	■ Set up opportunities for the team to get to know each other ■ Develop a clear purpose for the team ■ Agree objectives and outcomes for the team and individuals
Storming	■ Lack of clarity around roles ■ Conflict and misunderstanding around each other's role and approach ■ Lack of clarity around team leadership ■ Issues around communication and information sharing	■ Stop and review the process of how you are working together ■ Focus on building trust and understanding ■ Recognise and manage conflict
Norming	■ Setting up agreement around roles and ways of working ■ Being clear about expectations and deliverables ■ Creating commonly agreed ways of working	■ Develop clear review processes ■ Create a team charter and agree ways of working together ■ Initiate team development activities to help members understand each other
Performing	■ Becoming complacent ■ Ensuring that creativity is maintained ■ Being responsive to change and ideas from outside the team	■ Constantly review progress and analyse how the team is working ■ Provide regular feedback to each other

Table 6.3 continued

Stages	Possible Issues	Suggested Approaches
	■ Being aware that any change in the team make-up or wider environment can take the team back to one of the earlier stages	■ Maintain an environment of high support and high challenge ■ Bring in people from outside to challenge and develop ideas ■ Constantly review the process of how the team is working and performing
Adjourning	■ The team splits up ■ Sadness and confusion about 'what next' ■ Ensuring that success is recognised ■ Ensuring that team members are recognised for their achievements	■ Mark the occasion by celebrating achievements with the team and key stakeholders ■ Review learning and achievement on an individual and team basis and provide feedback to other parts of the business if appropriate ■ Provide support for team members in planning the next stages in their careers

Other issues can also create complexity in the team. Working on problems which don't have a definable solution or in partnerships with other organisations which have their own cultural perspectives can create difficulties. Add to this the generational and personality differences between team members and you have a real melting pot of values, approaches and team challenges.

Self-assessment Complexity Factors in Your Team

Complexity Factors	Present
Multicultural	
Multidisciplinary	
Multigenerational	
Geographically dispersed	
Home based or teleworking	
More than one time zone	
Cross-organisational, e.g. joint ventures, partnering	
Virtual, i.e. never meeting up	

Look at the self-assessment box above. Tick the types of complexity which are present in your team:

If you ticked three or more boxes, you are working in a complex team. Complex teams are hybrids, and like a highly-tuned sports car they need careful attention to ensure that they are operating at their full potential.

Case study

Sue manages a global research team. The team only meets once a year and conference calls and emails are the main form of interaction. One group email she sent produced a backlash from one country and looking back, Sue realised how it may have offended certain cultures. She then understood how important her interface with the team was. Sue needed to think more carefully about wording emails, sometimes sending individual rather than group ones, and building up positive communication relationships. Unlike a traditional office environment there was little opportunity to discuss misunderstandings. Sue needed to prevent the problems arising rather than sort them out later.

What Impact does the Organisation and Environment have on your Team?

The business environment has changed dramatically over recent years (see Table 6.4).

Cross-functional working, matrix structures and multiple team working mean that often, as a team leader, you are heading a group of people who don't directly report to you. These people will also have other priorities and will probably be contributing to other teams, so your role is one of motivating and influencing often without direct authority. To further complicate the situation, the pace of technology and complexity of task mean that you cannot be the expert. You must recognise that your contribution is that of leading, coaching and creating an environment where you can all succeed.

Table 6.4 Recent changes in the business environment

Changes in the Team Environment over the Past 10 Years	
From	**To**
Functional	Cross-functional
Multi-layered organisation structure	De-layered organisation structure
Relatively slow pace of change	Faster pace of change
A single work area	Multiple dispersed work areas
A single team	Working/contributing to many teams
Monocultural	Multicultural
Relatively simple communication	Greater variety and speed of communication
Technology-poor environment	Technology-rich environment, enabling multiple communication channels and knowledge sharing
Expertise in task	Expertise in process
A single boss	Multiple lines of reporting
A few stakeholders	Multiple stakeholders

Analysing Your Own Team

Use the Self-assessment box below to reflect on the type of team you are working in and use it to get the most out of this and the following chapters.

Self-assessment Identifying Your Team Type

Team Dimensions	Your Team	Areas to Focus On
Team type What type of team are you working in, i.e. a steady state team or *ad hoc* project-based team?		Whatever structure your team has it is important to get the basics right, so focus on the section on **Reasons for Team Failure** in this Chapter, Chapter 8 on **Team Leadership** and Chapter 7 on **Team Tools**.
Team size Less than 5 may need injection of creativity. More than 8 may necessitate creation of sub-teams.		Team size is important to consider especially in terms of some of the **Team Tools** concerned with communication and ways of working together.

Team Dimensions	Your Team	Areas to Focus On
Stages of team development What stage of development is your team at? Forming Norming Storming Performing Adjourning		Chapter 7 on **Team Tools** will be particularly useful as you can apply specific tools to the development stage of your team. Your leadership style will also need to develop as the team evolves, so look at leadership flexibility in **Team Leadership**, Chapter 8.
Levels of team complexity What types of complexity is influencing your team? Multicultural Multidisciplinary Multigenerational Geographic/time zones Home working Virtual teams		You will need to apply the techniques and approaches from the next few chapters to your own specific situation but remember that these techniques are all the more important if you don't have the luxury of face-to-face interaction.

Self-assessment Identifying Your Team Type

Team Dimensions	Your Team	Areas to Focus On
Organisational/ environmental issues What specific issues are affecting your role as a team leader and the success of your team?		Pay particular attention to the leadership skills and competences in **Leadership** and the section on **Managing Upwards and Outwards** in Chapter 8.

Summary

Remember the first stage in developing your team involves understanding just what type of group you are working with. Teamwork isn't a 'one size fits all approach', so ensure that you take the time to analyse what type of team you are leading.

- Understand the complexities your team faces.
- Understand the environmental issues which may impact on the way your team works.
- If your team is not working effectively, identify whether any of the five possible reasons for failure is affecting your unit.

Once you have looked at these issues, focus on the tools outlined in the next chapter which will help to accelerate the overall success and development of your team.

Developing Your Team Tool Kit

Teamwork doesn't happen by magic. Think of your favourite sports team; success for them takes time. It is built from selecting talented team members who have a very clear goal. They learn to work well together, understand each other's strengths, respect each other, create winning strategies, work with their coach, review their performance, learn from mistakes and achieve results.

All high-performing teams have similar characteristics and your role as a team leader is to build an environment which nurtures these traits. We recognise that you probably don't have the luxury of selecting the most talented people, or even members whose sole focus is on your team. Often now, people work for a number of teams and are juggling an array of conflicting objectives. However, the Self-assessment questionnaire below can help you to think about whether you have the right ingredients in place to create a successful group.

You can answer these questions as a way of reflecting on your team's performance or use them with the team as a way of gaining feedback and identifying your team strengths and areas for improvement

---

Self-assessment Clarifying Team Ingredients for Success

Purpose and vision	**Yes**	**No**

1. Is the team vision clear to all team members?
2. Is the team aware of its purpose and objectives?
3. Do you have buy-in from all of the stakeholders?
4. Does the team have a clear focus on outcomes and deliverables?

Overall on a scale of 1 to 10 (where 1 is low and 10 is high), how clear are you on the team vision and purpose?
Your score:

Performance

1. Do all team members have clear roles/responsibilities and accountabilities?

	Yes	No

2. Is progress measured and reviewed on a regular basis?

3. Do team members receive regular feedback on their performance

4. Has the team developed effective ways of working together?

Overall on a scale of 1 to 10, are you satisfied with the way performance is managed in the team?

Your score:

Relationships

1. Do team members understand and respect each other?

2. Is there a high degree of trust amongst the team?

3. Is conflict in the team dealt with in a positive manner?

4. Does the team review the process of how they work together on a regular basis?

Overall on a scale of 1 to10, how would you rate the quality of relationships in the team?

Your score:

Communication

1. Are a range of communication tools used by the team?

2. Does everyone in the team have the opportunity to contribute ideas?

3. Is there regular communication within the team and with external stakeholders?

4. Has the team agreed common practices for communication and exchanging information?

Overall on a scale of 1 to 10, how effective is team communication?

Your score:

Learning	Yes	No
1. Is the team encouraged to learn from its experience?		
2. Are team members stretched and challenged?		
3. Do team members have the opportunity to set and develop individual development objectives?		
4. Do team members receive coaching and development?		
Overall on a scale of 1 to10, how valuable is the learning experience of working in this team?		
Your score:		

If you and the team answered 'yes' to all the questions, congratulations. However, be aware that teams are fluid and dynamic, and positive areas can change on a regular basis. All you need are some shifting goalposts, changes in team dynamics or extra pressures from outside and this equilibrium can be upset. You need to work with the team so that they can review and develop their performance both as individuals and as a group in order to maintain your current success.

If you answered 'no' to some of the questions, don't despair, as there are plenty of practical things you can do to improve performance and accelerate the development of your team.

The Self-assessment questionnaire has been developed around a model for high-performing teams and a selection of techniques to help in the areas shown in Figure 7.1 follow.

The four areas of purpose, performance, relationships and communication are the cornerstones of effective team work. However, a high standard in one alone is not sufficient for good results. If you have a clear purpose but poor relationships your team will be unlikely to achieve its goal. It is the synergy between these four elements which is the key to success.

Team learning is at the centre of the model because it is part and parcel

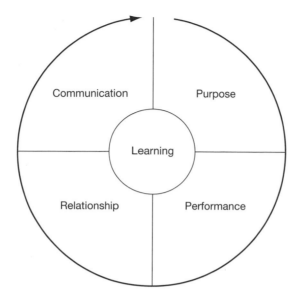

Figure 7.1   High-performing teams

of each segment. Without clear performance goals, shared purpose, quality relationships and effective communication team members will not have the opportunity to grow as individuals or as a team.

These factors are common to all teams but how they are implemented may differ depending on the make-up and type of group you are working with.

Purpose

Being clear about the purpose of the team is essential. It provides the practical clarity which you need to move ahead. It must be shared, agreed and created with the involvement of the team and other stakeholders (who may have their own views on how to proceed).

The purpose underlines the whole reason that the team is in existence and is especially important for new teams coming together. However, with more established groups, purpose is something which needs to be revisited and reviewed on a regular basis.

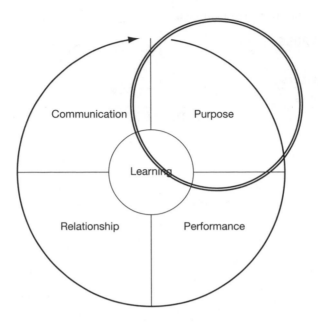

Figure 7.2 High-performing teams: purposes

The purpose of a team should include:

- The **key objectives.**
- Who the **members of the team** are.
- Who the **key stakeholders** are.
- The critical success factors or **inputs** that the team requires from the organisation and each other to succeed.
- The key deliverables described in terms of **outcomes.**
- The financial and non-financial **benefits** which will be delivered during the activities, and on completion of the task.

Identifying the critical success factors or inputs is particularly important, as these need to be in place in order for the team to achieve its objective – and they need to be agreed at the outset.

Table 7.1 provides a framework to use with your team to gain a common understanding of what you want to achieve.

Table 7.1   Team purpose framework

TEAM PURPOSE		
Objective		
Team members		
Stakeholders		
INPUTS	OUTCOMES	BENEFITS

Inviting all the key stakeholders to sign this off is very important as it establishes their buy-in and their commitment to provide the resources you need to succeed.

Case study

Rosemary was asked to set up a temporary team to help implement a new sales and marketing IT system. The system had been designed to capture important sales data and ensure that trends and market intelligence could be quickly and easily accessed by other areas of the business.

Rosemary reported to the Director of training and development, but would be working closely with the IT department who were responsible for the implementation. Her team of seven, were drawn from different parts of the business and were all individuals who had expressed an interest in championing the new system.

The first thing Rosemary did was to pull the team together and establish the common purpose. Together they worked on the purpose chart illustrated below.

Team purpose   To support the implementation of the new sales and marketing system

Objective   To train 150 managers across the business to use the new IT system by December

Team members   Paul, Sally, Simone, Raj, Colin, Pat, Sue

Stakeholders   IT Director, Director of training and development, Head of sales and marketing, Divisional directors, Financial Director

Inputs	Outcomes	Benefits
■ Systems and delivery training for the core team. ■ Team members to be released from their current role for 50% of their time over the next 6 months. ■ Mandatory for managers to attend training. ■ Budget to cover travel and expenses. ■ IT equipment. ■ Training facilities on site.	■ 150 managers able to use the system to input sales data and market intelligence on a monthly basis. ■ End of month sales figures to be produced within 90% accuracy within 2 days of month end.	■ Sales managers more involved in the business. ■ Easing the workload of the finance department in collating month end information. ■ Creating the ability to analyse trends and respond to market conditions with greater speed and accuracy.

It was only when Rosemary drew up this chart with her team that she realised the number of stakeholders involved and the need to ensure commitment to provide the necessary inputs to achieve the task. The team were also very clear about what they needed to achieve and how they would be able to measure their success. It also meant that they were able to discuss how best to achieve the task and how to support each other through the coming months.

Performance

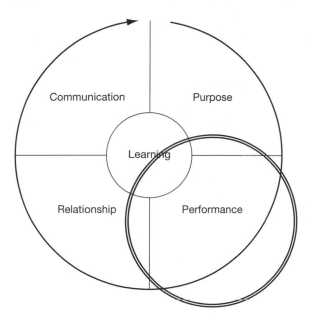

Figure 7.3   High-performing teams: performance

Once the purpose has been set and agreed by all parties the next stage is to focus on team performance. The previous section defined the required outcomes. This section looks at how to reach those outcomes by agreeing team accountabilities and responsibilities, ways of working together to

Figure 7.4   The performance pyramid

achieve your purpose, and finally setting some clear, focused objectives to ensure that the team is able to achieve its overall objectives (see Figure 7.4).

Why Focus on Outcomes?

Focusing on outcomes both at a team and individual level has a number of advantages:

1. It keeps the team focused on the end result and creates a shared understanding around the overall purpose.
2. It provides clarity in what you want to measure.
3. It provides freedom for the team to think about how they want to achieve their goals.
4. It can help to manage team time. If everyone keeps asking themselves how what they are doing is helping to achieve the overall outcome they are less likely to spend time on unproductive areas of work.

> ### Case study
>
> For Rosemary's team their outcome was to ensure that 150 managers in the business were able to input the relevant data into the system on a monthly basis. Another outcome was that the monthly sales figures for the business would be produced within 90% accuracy within 2 days of month end. This certainly provided a clear outcome and also helped the team think about how they could measure success and monitor the accuracy of the figures over coming months. This would in turn highlight any areas where they needed to provide support to managers who for some reason were finding it difficult to input their data.

Once you have a clear end result in mind, you can work with the team to create some specific outcomes and milestones along the way. A good way of doing this is to create a time line. Imagine a line on the floor representing the team as it moves through time. Ask the team members to walk down their time line identifying different milestones along the way until they get to the end of the project, or to an agreed time slot in the future.

Ask them to imagine what would be happening if everything had gone well. What would have been achieved? What would customers and other key stakeholders be saying? What would be happening differently in the organisation and externally?

Case study

Rosemary's team were able to identify a number of milestones:

1. *Their training in the system and ways of delivering it to the target audience*
2. *The development of training and support materials*
3. *Pilot session and review*
4. *Role out of the training*
5. *Monitoring of the outcomes to measure the success of the training*
6. *Additional sessions to support and coach managers*
7. *Review of overall progress, performance review and feedback for team members*

As you can see, once you have agreed the milestones and outcomes along the way you can plan some timeframes, and go on to identify individual accountabilities and responsibilities. Doing this with the team means that they will be able to shape the process and understand how to support other team members to achieve the overall objective.

Accountabilities

Once the outcomes have been identified it is important to agree individual and team accountabilities and responsibilities. Identifying who is accountable for the different aspects of the team's work is central to its success and creates a feeling of shared responsibility. Team members may be individually accountable for achieving their contribution or they may need to work with others.

> *Case study*
>
> *With Rosemary's team each member had individual account-ability for the business area they were championing. She allocated different roles to different team members (i.e. development of materials, measuring feedback and implementation, setting up the training schedule and resourcing the programmes) However, they had mutual accountability for the success of the training and the overall business result.*

When you are setting accountabilities, remember to include your stake-holders. They can help to provide valuable input and resources for the team and act as gatekeepers to ensure that the outcomes can be achieved.

Ways of Working

When the outcomes and accountabilities have been agreed the team can focus on deciding how to work together effectively. These ways of working need to be clearly established and can cover areas such as:

- The frequency and types of meetings.
- Feedback and review of individual team performance.
- How to handle disagreements.
- When and how to celebrate success.
- Response times to emails and requests.
- Support that team members give each other.
- Training and development requirements.
- The ways in which information is communicated and shared.
- Expectations from each other and from the team leader.
- The amount of time team members can give to the team.
- Working hours.

This does take a fair aount of time but it is well worth the effort as it means that everyone understands how the team will be operating and gives a firm foundation for working together in the future.

> **Case study**
>
> *In Rosemary's case, the team decided that they would have a weekly teleconference to review their progress and highlight any problems. They also agreed that they would work with different team members so that they could share their approaches to training and delivery and understand different parts of the business. They wanted to monitor the effectiveness of the training both at the end of the session and also a month down the line to ensure that managers were happy with the system. To do this they agreed to set up some telephone coaching and feedback so that they could provide ongoing support.*

Team and Individual Objectives

Once you have worked through the outcomes, accountabilities and ways of working you are ready to agree some specific objectives with your team. You are also in a position to identify any specific training and development needs at either an individual or team level.

Whilst the process of setting objectives is familiar to most managers it is important to be aware of how the environment we work in is influencing the whole process of performance management.

Traditionally objectives are set each year and reviewed at least on a half-yearly basis with the line manager. However, the unpredictability of our business environment means that the goalposts are often changing. As a result, objectives need to be fluid and regularly changed and adapted to the new circumstances. In addition, as team members are often working in more matrix-type structures, it is important to gain feedback from other sources about their performance. The growth in numbers of 'Generation Y' in the workforce (see Chapter 2) means that the review process needs to take in the whole person and take account of development needs. There is also a stronger focus now on the 'soft' objectives. These refer to 'how' the job is done, not just the results. They reflect competences such as customer service, coaching, communication and team involvement. These more behavioural objectives are vitally important for

Table 7.2 Traditional and new approaches in the business environment

Traditional Approach	New Approach
Objectives set on an annual basis.	Objectives are flexible and are likely to change during the year.
Reviews held twice a year.	Performance is reviewed on an ongoing basis.
Focus on measurable hard objectives.	Focus on hard and soft objectives.
Focus on the job.	Focus on the role and the whole person.
Focus on activities.	Focus on outcomes.
Focus on achievements.	Focus on achievement and development.
Feedback on performance comes directly from the manager.	Feedback comes from multiple sources.
Performance reviews are always face-to-face meetings.	Performance reviews can be conducted face-to-face or virtually.

team performance as members need to be working together in order to achieve overall success.

Take a look at Table 7.2 and analyse whether the traditional approach is still appropriate for your team or whether you need to adopt any of the new approaches listed in the right hand column.

Case study

Rosemary didn't line manage any of her people, but she was responsible for their performance whilst they worked in the temporary implementation team. Because of the nature of the work she set performance objectives at the beginning of the project and reviewed them on a bi-monthly basis, and at the close of the project. (Some of these reviews were conducted virtually as the team were working in different divisions.) Because the outputs had been clarified it was easy to access the hard data to measure success in areas such as the number of managers implementing the new system, and the degree of accuracy with which they used it. There were also some very important soft objectives such as the level of customer service, training style, and the attitude of team members. These could be measured by feedback from managers attending the training event and also feedback from any ongoing coaching and support. This meant that whilst Paula didn't see the team on a regular basis she was able to review their performance and provide support where needed. The feedback from the review was also communicated to the individual's line manager so that they could appreciate the input their team member had made in championing the new system.

The message here is that you need to tailor your performance review process to the environment you are operating in and ensure that you are able to set up a measurement process which reflects the outcomes and objectives you want to achieve.

Relationships

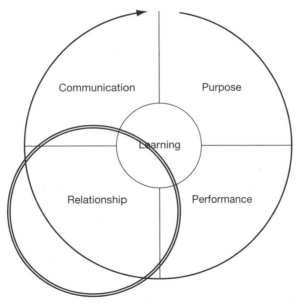

Figure 7.5   High-performing teams: relationships

Whilst the task might drive the team, the relationships are the lubricant that ensures that creativity, quality and customer satisfaction are achieved. For a team to be high performing there needs to be trust, understanding of each other's roles and personalities, openness and mutual respect.

This is easier said than done and it rarely happens by itself. High-performing teams need the opportunity to work on these issues in a planned way so that they can develop and grow. Team leaders who ignore this element will often end up with situations where team members compete with each other, conflict goes unresolved and there is a reluctance to support others and make that extra effort.

The three main areas which can help in the process of building relationships are: Building trust, Feedback and review and Managing conflict. It is worth remembering that you can work on these issues at the same time as focusing on the task at hand.

Building Trust

Building trust takes time and often happens in stages as people get to know each other. In face-to-face teams, trust is built by working together in the same time and space. This enables team members to develop shared values, empathy and a confidence to predict each other's behaviour and reactions.

With virtual teams the process of building trust is different. It needs to be established at the outset. The first interactions between team members are crucial to success. So, if you are managing a virtual team, remember that it is important to set the right tone from the beginning.

There are three common factors in developing trust in virtual teams. The first is to start off building up social knowledge amongst team members, in other words help the team to get to know each other. The second involves setting and agreeing clear roles and responsibilities. The third factor is to display a positive attitude; to keep interactions supportive, enthusiastic and upbeat.

There are plenty of ways to start off the process of building trust and it is an important element in the early stages of team development. The first stage is helping the team to get to know each other. Team members need the opportunity to share something about who they are and what they do at the very early stages of working together. Even if your team does not have the opportunity to meet face-to-face you can ask them each to develop a Powerpoint slide depicting

- Who they are.
- What they do.
- How they like to work.
- What they would like to get out of working in this team.

The question about how they like to work is particularly important for cross-cultural groups. Some cultures prefer to discuss and agree the way forward, other cultures want their boss to tell them what to do and other more individualistic cultures just want to get on with it. In addition, if your team is dispersed, members may have different working routines. Some may be happy to be contacted 24/7 whilst others may be trying to work round other commitments.

Another way of building trust is to develop a greater understanding of each other's personality and preferred style of working. There is a range of team-based questionnaires and psychometric instruments which can help team members understand how to work together more effectively. Some of the most widely used are MBTI (Myers Briggs Type Inventory) and the Belbin team questionnaire.

Any common learning experience, even on-line collaborative learning and team meetings, can provide the opportunity to build trust. As a leader, it is important to look at any occasion not just as a way of getting work done but as a way of building relationships as evidence shows that teams with higher levels of trust will deliver better results.

Tips for Success

- Allow the time and space for the team to get to know each other.
- Ensure that clear roles and responsibilities are shared between team members.
- Encourage team members to deliver on their agreements as confidence in each others work helps to build trust.
- Use a team questionnaire to understand more about each others style and approach.
- Explore differences and concerns rather than letting things bottle up
- Do some team training together.
- Celebrate successes and encourage an environment where feedback is welcomed.

Feedback and Review

Trust is also developed as team members feel more confident and able to provide feedback to each other. This not only helps individuals develop their skills and confidence but it also enhances the ability for the team to review how they are working together and what they need to do to improve their performance.

The skills of one-to-one feedback are covered in Chapter 3. You can further develop these skills by applying them to the process of reviewing team performance. Here are a few ideas.

1. At the beginning of a meeting allow time for each team member to provide feedback on their progress and give an update on what they are doing. This need not take long but it allows each person a chance to get their voice heard and share what they have achieved since the last meeting.
2. Equally at the end of any meeting or telephone conference take the time to review:
   - How the meeting went
   - How we are working as a team.
   - What we could do more/less of.
   - What we need to do to improve future meetings.

High support

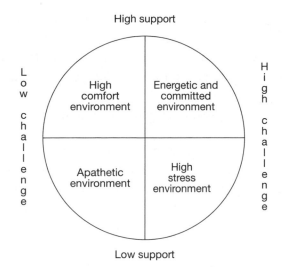

Low support

Figure 7.6 The support and challenge model

This has the added advantage of improving the quality and pro-ductivity of future meetings.

3. Another useful review tool is the Support and challenge model, Figure 7.6. Ask team members to identify where they see the team on the support and challenge matrix above. Use this to discuss what they need to do to move into the top right hand box of high support and high challenge.

To move to the high support and high challenge quarter requires team members to:
- Listen well to each other.
- Question and develop ideas.
- Challenge ideas in order to develop and create an even better outcome.
- Respect and understand each other.
- Appreciate the strengths each member brings to the team.

This model can be used to provide feedback and identify ways of devel-oping levels of trust and team performance in order to operate effectively in the top right hand quarter.

Whilst feedback on the way the group is working is important in high-per-forming teams, it will also create an environment where members feel comfortable giving feedback to each other and to their team leader. As a leader, receiving feedback on what you are doing well and what the team would like you to do differently can be very valuable. In fact, it will make your life a whole lot easier if you know what your team needs from you rather than trying to second guess them. The same goes for team members, who sometimes may not appreciate what their colleagues need from them.

An easy way to do this is to ask what team members appreciate about your performance and what they would like to see change or develop for the future. This can be done either face-to-face or on line. If you want the responses to be anonymous you can ask your HR department to collate the results for you.

However, nothing beats face-to-face feedback. If you haven't had these sorts of conversations with your team it may feel a bit awkward to begin with, but once people get started it can open up ways of helping team members to build their skills and capabilities.

Managing Conflict

Whilst trust is an important feature of any high-performing team so too is the ability to manage and work effectively with conflict.

The first thing to remember about conflict is that it isn't a bad thing to have around. If handled well, conflict can lead to better ideas with greater commitment and ownership. However, if handled badly, it can lead to poor relationships, low morale and lack of team collaboration, with consequences for bottom line performance.

Some of the typical reasons for team conflict are issues of role ambiguity, interdependencies between people, personality differences and differences in views and values. With this in mind the previous sections focusing on Purpose and Performance are especially important in creating role clarity.

An important aspect of team leadership is to understand how to create an environment where conflict can be positively handled and to develop some tools and techniques to ensure that the team have the capability to use conflict as a positive force for creativity and performance.

Look at the situation below.

> ### Case study
>
> *A group of managers came together as a team to review the performance management processes in their organisation and create one system which could reward excellent performance. The managers came from different areas of the business, and had different views on what should be rewarded and how. They also had different views on the role of financial reward in motivating people. Finally, they had their own hidden agendas as the system would certainly affect them in different ways. In addition, they all had different personalities, some much stronger and more vocal than others.*

It is easy to imagine a scenario where different departmental and personal perspectives could lead to a conflict spiral – disagreement on views, lots of ideas being proposed, heated debate, people getting emotionally involved in the argument trying to fight their own corner and, finally, a situation where no agreement is reached or, worse still, an agreement that doesn't have everyone's buy-in. This is then implemented poorly because of the lack of commitment from the team members.

What could the team leader have done to avoid this happening? What could be done to create a more positive outcome?

What happened in reality was that the team leader was able to work with the different agendas and approaches.

Case study

The managers planned a process for the meeting whereby team members had the opportunity to view their concerns and ideas about the new system. At one stage the meeting got stuck, with a seemingly insoluble situation. This was a turning point which could have led to an impasse at best, and a major disagreement at worst. Recognising this, the team leader stopped the meeting, expressed her concerns and frustrations, and asked each member to summarise their current thoughts and feelings. The result was that this took the meeting to a more strategic level where the team members went on to identify the key behaviours, attitudes and aspects of performance which they wanted to encourage and develop in the workforce. Once they had agreed this common vision, it was far easier to move ahead and develop a process which had a clear corporate focus and met the overall needs of each department.

So what are the lessons from this?

- Allow people time to consider and voice their views.
- Give people individual time to tell their story so that you can understand their perspective.
- Gain buy-in to an overall common goal or focus.
- Be clear about the big picture before you go into the details.
- Listen to all views.
- Be prepared to stop and review when you feel the meeting is reaching an impasse. (It's often good to have a break at this time to allow people to reflect.)
- Labelling your feelings is much more powerful than expressing them emotionally, i.e. the team leader stated that she felt frustrated rather than showing it emotionally through her voice and body language.
- It is worth remembering that if you maintain rapport with someone you are far more likely to have a discussion than a heated conflict.

Recognising people's personal and cultural approach to conflict

Something you can do with your team is to explore and recognise each other's approach to managing conflict. There are a number of different conflict handling styles and approaches, all of which can be useful in different situations.

Table 7.3 identifies five different conflict modes which were identified by Thomas Kilman. Details of his questionnaire are provided in the Conclusion section.

1. Competing – the goal is to win.
2. Collaborating – the goal is to find a win-win solution.
3. Compromising – the goal is to find a middle ground.
4. Avoiding – the goal is to delay.
5. Accommodating – the goal is to fit in.

Looking at the list above, can you identify your own preference? As you can see all the styles have their advantages, but need to be used in the right situation. Using the wrong style may mean that the conflict escalates, or that people leave the situation feeling very unhappy about the decision being made.

Recognising your preferences and those of the team can help members understand each other and identify the consequences of their approach. It also enables the team to develop ways of managing potential conflict and identifying any patterns they may fall into.

Table 7.3 Five conflict handling modes

Style	Key Skills	Positive Use	Potential Problems
Competing	– ability to argue and debate – ability to use rank and influence – standing your ground – stating your position clearly	– when quick action is required – when you know you are right – to protect yourself from people who take advantage of non-competitive behaviour	– people may be afraid to challenge to you – this style may be demotivational as it doesn't involve others
Collaborating	– listening – non-threatening confrontation – analysing input – identifying concerns	– when both sets of concerns are important – when you want to learn from other people's viewpoint – finding a solution which satisfies both parties	– it takes time to discuss the issues – it needs to be reciprocated by others for it to work – can lead to work overload – others may take advantage and responsibility for action may be unclear
Compromising	– negotiating – finding the middle ground – making concessions – assessing value	– can achieve a temporary settlement – if two groups have equal power and are equally committed to their goal	– no one is happy – a poor solution is agreed – it can create a lack of trust and feeling of game playing

Table 7.3   continued

Style	Key Skills	Positive Use	Potential Problems
Avoiding	– ability to withdraw – sidestepping – sense of timing – ability to leave things unresolved	– if the issue is unimportant – if there is no chance of satisfying your concerns – if you need time to let the situation cool down	– it ignores others' concerns – decisions may be made by default – lack of input from you – issues may fester and build up
Accommodating	– listening and understanding – keeping the peace – creating goodwill – foregoing your own desires	– when you realise that you are wrong – when the issue is more important to the other person than yourself – when you want to preserve harmony	– you may be neglecting your own concerns for those of others – you defer too much to the concerns of others – your ideas may not get the attention they deserve

Adapting to cultural differences

Different cultures have different approaches to handling conflict and it is important to recognise and discuss these. For example, in some of the Far Eastern countries the concept of 'face' is very important. It is not acceptable to openly disagree with or criticise someone. This means that conflict is not voiced in the same way as it is in the West. Also, in many cultures, disagreeing with people who are more senior than you is taboo.

Some cultures are also more direct in how they voice conflict. One Swedish manager I worked with talked about how hard it was to understand his British colleagues. The manager was used to being very direct and straightforward and found the British approach too vague; he wasn't sure whether people agreed with his ideas or not.

If you are working in a multicultural group, it is well worth spending some time discussing approaches and ways of dealing with conflict, and agreeing some common ground rules and ways of working together to ensure that everyone's views can be considered.

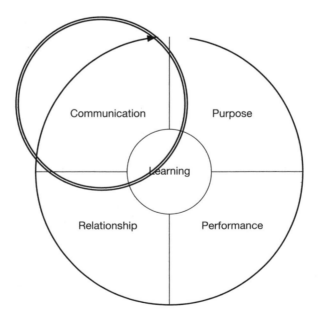

Figure 7.7   High-performing teams: communication

Communication

So, building trust, establishing feedback and review processes and managing conflict are three key areas in developing team relationships. They could not happen without clear communication.

Communication is the glue which holds the team together. If the team is communicating well, relationships will flourish, trust will develop and more creative ideas will emerge. If this is happening, the chances are that you will be operating as a high-performing team.

This is not about the frequency of meetings and the quantity of information sent out. The key to effective communication lies in the quality of the interactions. These govern the overall effectiveness of the communication tools used.

As a team leader you need to be aware of how your team operates and whether the communication tools and processes you use are appropriate. As teams become more complex so too does the way in which they communicate.

Table 7.4 illustrates some of the ways in which team communication is changing.

Table 7.4 Changes in the ways teams communicate

From	To
■ Face-to-face.	■ Virtual communication and teleconferences.
■ Regular meetings together.	■ Infrequent meetings together.
■ Corridor conversations.	■ Remote conversations.
■ Email.	■ Range of technologies from chat rooms, instant messenger to collaborative technologies.
■ One language and culture.	■ Multicultural.

Different time	Shift and rota team	Geographically dispersed/ different time zone
Same time	Face-to-face team	Geographically dispersed/ same time zone

Same place   Different place

Task

Figure 7.8   Team communication

Adapted from *Managing Virtual Teams*, Joe Willmore, Spiro Business Press, 2003.

It is worth thinking about your team and assessing whether you are using the right tools and techniques. One way of doing this is to identify where your team is in Figure 7.8.

Same time/same place

Your team will have the luxury of seeing each other on a regular basis and the most appropriate ways of communicating will be meetings, corridor conversations, email and telephone. Your challenges will be around ensuring that meetings are really adding value and that the team has the opportunity to develop and work together effectively.

Same time/different place

In this situation, your team will be geographically dispersed but working in the same time zone, e.g. a sales team spread across the region. The luxury of face-to-face meetings will be replaced by a greater reliance on emails and teleconferences. Your challenge as a team leader will often be to balance the pressures on your time due to the amount of travel involved and the need to disseminate information and communicate virtually with team members

Different time/same place

This type of format will be characterised by teams who operate on a shift or rota system, such as medical care teams. The key challenges here will be how to pass on information, update colleagues and provide feedback. The importance of technology in terms of shared folders and information updating and transfer are vitally important.

Different time/different place

These teams will not only be geographically dispersed but working across different time zones. The pressures of communication and travel will mean that leaders (and team members) will often face the challenge of being available 24/7. There will be a real need in this environment to develop and use more collaborative online tools, manage across cultures and show respect for other people's life styles and working patterns.

Team leaders frequently face problems due to overreliance on face-to-face communication, which can often lead to burn-out as result of constant travel and 24/7 working. It's well worth reappraising how you work and remembering that with effective communication, trust can be developed virtually.

Whatever type of team you are working in there are some common tools and techniques which need to be honed, in order for the team to work to its potential. You also need to develop a clear communication strategy so that you can ensure you are making the most out of the communication opportunities available and using your time to best effect.

Making the Most of the Communication Tools Available

Whilst there are a growing number of communication options available, the following focus will be on the three most widely used: face-to-face meetings, teleconferences and emails, mainly because these tools, even though they have been around for quite a time, are rarely used effectively.

They form the backbone of most of the communication we use and provide the fabric for effective and positive team relationships.

Meeting skills

The first thing with meetings is to evaluate whether you are using them to their full potential. We all have experiences of sitting for hours in meetings which seem to be going nowhere and have little relevance to us.

So, first assess the value of your meetings:

- How often are they held?
- What is the purpose of the meeting?
- Is there a clear agenda and established chair?
- Are the relevant people present?
- Is everyone involved?
- Do you leave the meeting with clear outcomes and agreed actions?

If meetings are not seen as an efficient communication tool:

- Would it be easier to circulate a weekly newsletter if the objective is to update people on what is happening?
- Would it be better to use shared folders or communicate on-line if the objective is to update people on information and progress?
- Would it be better to see people on a one-to-one or small group basis if the objective is to deal with specific issues and problems?

Teleconference skills

A teleconference can be a complete disaster if it is not managed well. We've probably all experienced the situation where you are not sure who else is in the meeting, no one seems to have the relevant information to hand and people leave the conversation confused and frustrated.

If you want to build a team and establish your credibility as a team leader it is vitally important to make these meetings work, so here are a few tips.

Tips for Success

- Send out agendas and all material well in advance.
- Provide time beforehand to plan.
- Agree that everyone will give their full attention.
- Turn off all other devices (yes, those Blackberries).
- Sit somewhere where you don't have any distractions. Some managers find it best to face a blank wall.
- Make sure that everyone introduces themselves and new members have the opportunity to describe their role.
- Agree the agenda/outcomes and timeframe for the meeting.
- Check that all voices are heard and bring in quieter members of the team.
- Summarise progress on a regular basis so everyone knows what is happening.
- Be aware of cultural differences and of the fact that some of the members of team may not be using their first language. This means that you will need to give people time to think through their answers and ensure that everyone is speaking clearly.
- At the end of the meeting, review how the meeting could be improved for next time.
- Ensure that actions and outcomes are circulated immediately.

Email skills

We all have a love/hate relationship with email. It's a fantastic way to communicate and provides a record of your interaction, but it can take up an enormous amount of time sifting through information and conversations which may not be relevant. Here are a few tips and reminders which might put you back on track.

Tips for Success

- Think about the information you need to send out – who really needs it and would it be better to store it in a shared folder so people can access it when they require it?
- Plan and prepare messages and consider the tone of your writing, especially if you are working in a dispersed team where the quality of your email interaction acts as a replacement for face-to-face conversations.
- If working crossculturally, think about the cultural etiquette. In some cultures the relationship is important whilst in others it is fine to keep the focus on the task.
- Manage your time – set aside time to do emails. They can act as an interruption and as any time management specialist will tell you, interruptions can waste about 20 minutes as you will have to refocus on the task you were doing.
- Agree email etiquette with the team – this means agreeing what is communicated, and focusing on issues such as expected response time and who should be copied in.

Making the Most of Other Forms of Communication

Technology is constantly developing and if you are working with a dispersed team, it is well worth keeping up to date with the field so that you can ensure you are making the best use of time.

One international organisation I worked in was making savings of over half a million pounds on their travel bill just by using on-line collaborative tools. It enabled the team, who were spread around the globe, to literally work 24/7 and reduce the time to market for their product by 6 months. They recognised that working in new ways without reliance on face-to-face meetings could be equally valuable.

Instant messenger can be a great way of firing off 'Thank you's' and 'How are you's' to team members spread across time zones as they sign in for the day. Chat rooms can also be a valuable way of swapping team gossip and working on problems. Blogs and wikis are also becoming more popular as ways of conversing and managing knowledge in the team.

However, if you want to use these tools, a word of warning – make sure that everyone is up to speed and comfortable with the technology. Ideally set some team training or a mini project getting everyone to participate in the new process. The last thing you want is to create something that only half the team can access.

Creating a Communication Strategy

With the plethora of communication tools available and the variety of team formats, it is important to create and agree a communication strategy. This means thinking about the Who, What, How and Why of communication. A good example of this is Christine, who was working on a partnership project.

Case study

Christine worked in a consultancy environment and was involved in a partnership with another organisation to deliver a major change initiative. Her team was very broad, consisting of her direct reports, a delivery team in the client organisation, and a range of associates and providers who were responsible for different aspects of the change process. The overall team involved in the project consisted of 150 people but whilst they all needed to be aware of the vision, purpose and progress of the project, many of the teams had discrete responsibilities.

How would you tackle this communication challenge?

Christine recognised that communication was key to her role as team leader and recognised that it represented about 70% of her time. Shared folders were used for different projects, a communications board was used to share general information, and an on-line site was developed so that all the people involved could receive up-to-date information. This was supported by weekly telephone conferences where any of the team could share their views and gain an update of what was a fast-moving project. Thirty minutes after the call, the minutes were posted on the site.

As well as providing up-to-date information, these systems reduced the pressure on email and also reduced the time Christine spent updating the many parties involved. Yet whilst supporting different forms of communication she also valued face-to-face team events.

Christine's line managers got together on a monthly basis to review their progress and assess the objectives they had to achieve. This was a collaborative process to help solve problems, gain support and monitor progress. In addition, other sub-group meetings were held; Christine gradually realised that she didn't need to be at all of them and that allowing the team to take ownership was important.

Given that the team was so large and dispersed Christine tried to build bridges, where relevant, across the teams by giving different people responsibility for different aspects of the project. In so doing she was creating a network of mutually dependent relationships.

A couple of large group meetings were held at the beginning and end of the project, to launch the event and build relationships. This gave the team the opportunity to get to know each other so that they could put faces to emails and understand the complexity of how the team was operating. The final meeting was very much a review and celebration of the project success, giving the team the opportunity to share their stories and evaluate the process and lessons of how they had worked together.

Whatever the format and size of your team, you should reflect on your communication strategy. On average this accounts for about 50% of leaders' time, so you need to make sure that for your own sake, and that of the team, you are using all the available communication channels to their best effect.

Doing it with the team – creating your communication charter

The example above illustrates the importance of planning your communication strategy and adapting it to the type of team you are working with. It is also valuable to create a communication charter with the team so that you can all agree on some key rules and ways of communicating effectively.

A typical communication charter should cover areas such as:

■ Agreement on face-to-face meetings: venue/frequency/length/who is invited.
■ Format of the meeting : social time/organisation/group work/agendas.
■ Your ten commandments for effective meetings (these will be particular to each team but may include things such as use of Blackberries, listening, no talking over, clear agenda focus, etc.).
■ Agreement on what is communicated and how.
■ Deadlines for circulation of material, before and after the meeting.
■ Response times to requests and emails.
■ Special requirements such as translators, etc.
■ Review processes to assess the quality and effectiveness of the meeting.

Doing this as a team ensures agreement and builds a sense of responsibility and ownership. The charter can be reviewed on a regular basis to develop the way you work and accommodate any changes.

The Virtual Element

The communication processes you use need to adapt and evolve to meet the needs of the team. A particular challenge that managers are facing is managing the virtual element of team communication. There are some very important communication skills and techniques which you need to be aware of if you are managing a virtual team.

Tips for Success

- Sharpen your non-visual skills. Chapter 3 describes how important it is to build rapport. In a virtual environment you don't have the advantage of visual communication so you need to focus on vocal elements. This means picking up all the verbal and vocal cues in the communication. Your listening skills need to pick up on what is being said but also on what is being missed out in the conversation. You also need to be aware of the pace and tone and what this might mean.
- Develop your questioning skills. If you are working over the telephone asking questions, building on ideas and probing not only show your interest but can provide extra information. Questioning is also an essential part of coaching and as a virtual team leader telephone coaching will be a key skill to develop in others.
- Keep in regular contact with your team and find excuses to keep in touch as they may be feeling quite isolated.
- Develop a regular drumbeat of communication so that the team can feel connected.
- Develop specific ways to build trust – use newsletters, chat time at the beginning of meetings and conversations to exchange information on how things are going and encourage people to talk about themselves.
- Look for opportunities to encourage cross-team communication such as giving team members different responsibilities which require them to work with others.
- Keep an appreciative approach. Teams will respond well to looking at what has been successful and what they could do to improve rather than having to constantly focus on what is wrong.

The Cross-cultural Element

Some of the issues around cross-cultural communication have been considered in the section on trust, pp. 138–9. Working across cultures can be fun, enlightening and frustrating. Whilst there has been lots of research in this area it is important not to make too many generalisations about cultures, given that people are much more mobile and often from more diverse family backgrounds than in the past. It is also important to remember that other environmental aspects, such as the professional and organisational culture, also play their part in shaping people's communication preferences.

However, there are some recognised issues around the 'dominant culture effect'. This is often evidenced in the language used in meetings. People speaking in their mother tongue have a definite advantage and may dominate the meeting. In addition, processes and ways of working may inhibit creativity. For example, some cultures such as those of the US and UK are quite individualistic, whilst others such as those of Thailand and China favour a more collective approach, where ideas are agreed together and where harmony is more important in the relationship. As you can imagine, this can create all sorts of misunderstandings especially when trying to make decisions.

One way to explore some of these differences is to use the questionnaire below.

Ask team members to complete the questions in the Self-assessment box and then chart the results on meta plan boards so that people can see the different responses. They can then discuss where the differences lie and explore ways of understanding each other and working together more effectively.

Self-assessment Cross-cultural Communication Questionnaire

For each question, circle the number which is closest to your own views in most situations.

1. The leader is responsible for taking decisions about the team's work

   Decisions should be made by reaching consensus with the whole team

1	2	3	4	5	6	7

2. Authority and respect are obtained by one's position and background

   Authority and respect are earned through one's achievements

1	2	3	4	5	6	7

---

3. Social talk and building personal relationships are essential for teamworking

I want the team to be businesslike, only discussing matters relevant to our task

| 1 | 2 | 3 | 4 | 5 | 6 | 7 |

4. We should make careful plans, thus minimising disturbances to our work

We should respond to changing conditions, accepting that there's much we can't control

| 1 | 2 | 3 | 4 | 5 | 6 | 7 |

5. I make precise appointments, and I expect them to be kept on time

Appointments are flexible, and can easily be changed as priorities shift

| 1 | 2 | 3 | 4 | 5 | 6 | 7 |

6. Conflict and personal feedback should be minimised, maintaining harmony in the team

Conflict should be confronted openly, and we should give direct feedback to people

| 1 | 2 | 3 | 4 | 5 | 6 | 7 |

7. Particular people or cases may require different approaches and solutions

We should have principles and standards which we apply consistently to all cases/people

| 1 | 2 | 3 | 4 | 5 | 6 | 7 |

8. We should be calm and objective at work: it's unprofessional to show our feelings

Expressing how we feel is important for working effectively together

| 1 | 2 | 3 | 4 | 5 | 6 | 7 |

9. I like competitive, high-achieving teams; I don't tolerate underperforming members

I like supportive, loyal teams; I accept that some members perform better than others

| 1 | 2 | 3 | 4 | 5 | 6 | 7 |

10. I like to have hard facts, and a clear and detailed structure, before I start work

I am comfortable about starting work even if there is much uncertainty and ambiguity

| 1 | 2 | 3 | 4 | 5 | 6 | 7 |

Based on the cross-cultural dimensions in the research models of Geert Hofstede (*Culture's Consequences*) and Fons Trompenaars (*Riding The Waves Of Culture*).

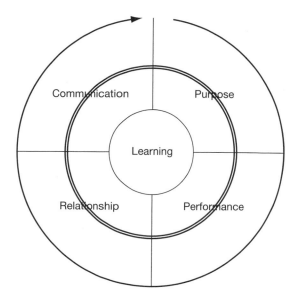

Figure 7.9 High-performing teams: learning

Learning

The final aspect of the team model is the central part, team learning. All high-performing teams learn and grow together. The techniques and skills covered so far in this chapter are all important to this process:

- A clear purpose will provide a focus for team and individual learning.
- Accountabilities, responsibilities and objectives can provide learning challenges for individual team members.
- Feedback and review at an individual and team level can help to improve performance.
- Positive relationships and good communication will enable team members to create an open climate where they can give feedback to each other and feel comfortable asking for help and support.

Whilst these elements will by their very nature ensure that learning is recognised in the team, there are a number of ways you can help the group and the individuals in it to maximise their development.

1. **Make sure that learning goals are explicit**
   When you are working with team members to set objectives, make sure that you spend time discussing their development needs and learning goals. Once you understand these you can delegate work which can help them develop, and also identify coaching opportunities along the way.

2. **Understand the different learning styles of team members**
   People learn in different ways and understanding each other's preferences can help a team to appreciate their own style and that of their colleagues. The four different learning styles originally identified by Peter Honey and Alan Mumford are: activist, reflector, theorist and pragmatist.

   > **The activist** is someone who likes to get involved in new experiences. They are action oriented and learn by doing. They are not afraid to have a go and tackle new challenges with enthusiasm
   >
   > **The reflector** is someone who prefers to reflect and think about what is happening. They like to stand back and look at a situation, gather data and will often listen to the views of others before offering their own ideas.
   >
   > **The theorist** is someone who likes to understand the underlying logic and theory behind what they are doing. They take an analytical approach and work through things step by step.
   >
   > **The pragmatist** is someone who likes to focus on practical outcomes and relevance to what they are doing. They like concepts which they can directly apply to their job.

   There are no right or wrong styles, but each has its own strengths and weaknesses. You may recognise your own approach and that of your team members from this brief description. As a result you can reflect on how to adapt your style to meet the learning needs of your people. For example, if you are primarily an activist you will need to allow time for the reflectors in your team to think things through in more detail. The theorists will want to check out the underlying logic and the pragmatists will be asking themselves how relevant what you are saying is to their specific issue. You can't expect everyone to leap straight into the problem in the same way you do!

3. **Conduct a team skills audit**
   One way of understanding the learning needs in your team is to conduct a skills audit. This is easily done by identifying all the key skills needed in the team and asking the members to identify their specific

strengths and development needs. Obviously all team members don't need to be proficient in all the skill areas, but you should be able to identify any overall skills gaps, and also be in a position to match up people who are skilled in a specific area with others who have identified it as a development need.

4. **Develop coaching across the team**

   Once you have identified the skills gaps and matched up experienced and inexperienced team members you can encourage the team to coach and develop each other. The skills of coaching and feedback were covered in Chapter 4 and it is important to remember that these are not just skills for a team leader, but can be used effectively by all team members. Your role can be one of developing a coaching ethos in the team so that individuals can develop their overall capability and potential.

5. **Encourage mentoring**

   Another way of helping to develop the skills of individual team members is to encourage them to find a mentor in the organisation. A mentor is usually someone who is more senior and in a different department or area of the business. Their role is to provide the individual with help and advice. This is particularly useful if your team is having to influence others and interact with other business areas, as the mentor can often provide insights and suggestions on how to manage the political and cultural aspects of their role.

6. **Implement some team-related training**

   Whilst individual training is useful, team-related training has the advantage of focusing on specific team issues, with the added bonus of bringing the group together. Product and technical training can be completed as a team. In addition, team-building events can help to reflect on progress and identify new, more effective ways of working together.

7. **Review team and individual learning**

   Finally, taking time to reflect on individual and team learning is as important as focusing on the task. If you are working in a temporary team this is the time to help individuals reflect on their development and think about what they need to do in the future. It is also an important part of completing any project, providing the opportunity to reflect on what the team and its members have learnt from the experience and to identify what they need to do differently to ensure success in the future.

Summary

Remember:

- There are four cornerstones to effective team work, Purpose, Performance, Relationships and Communication. Whatever type of team you are working with these elements are crucial to success and will enable it to learn and grow.
- You will need to select the techniques to fit the specific type of team you are working with, the people you are working with and the stage of team development you are operating at.
- The more complex your team, the more important it is to ensure that the four cornerstones of high-performance teamwork are developed and understood by your people
- Team learning is central to working as a high-performing team and time spent focusing on individual and team learning needs can help both develop and grow.

Team Leadership

Your approach to leadership has major consequences for the overall effectiveness of your team. To be an effective leader you need to be aware of your leadership style, recognise the implications of your actions *and* be able to understand how to alter your approach to get the most out of your team.

Team leaders also need to be adept at managing upwards and outwards. Managing your boss and recognising the needs of the stakeholders involved in your team's success is important. This is especially so given the fact that often managers are operating in environments where they have little direct authority and need to rely on their ability to influence others in order to achieve results.

Identifying and Developing Your Leadership Style

How would you describe your leadership style?
What do you see as your main leadership strengths?
How would others describe your approach?

These questions may provide you with some insight into your leadership style. Many managers operate on autopilot and just do what they think is best. In a busy environment there is little time to plan and even less time to review the effectiveness of our approach. Yet as a team leader you set the tone for the communication and environment in the group so it is important to take a few moments to reflect on the consequences of your actions.

Assessing Your Leadership Style

The questionnaire in the Self-assessment box below will help you to identify your style.

Think about each statement and rate yourself accordingly using the four-point scale below:

1. Never.
2. Sometimes.
3. Often.
4. Always.

Try to be as honest and objective as possible.

Circle one response for each item on the scale.

Take your time with each item and think about specific examples or situations you use that demonstrate the competency.

Self-assessment Assessing Your Leadership Style

1	I always provide clear direction.	1 2 3 4
2	I recognise the different skills and abilities of people in my team.	1 2 3 4
3	I spend time coaching team members.	1 2 3 4
4	I recognise and encourage creativity in the team.	1 2 3 4
5	I drive others to achieve performance targets.	1 2 3 4
6	I work with the team to agree ground rules and ways of working.	1 2 3 4
7	I motivate team members to perform to their potential.	1 2 3 4
8	I encourage team members to take initiative.	1 2 3 4
9	I am involved in the day-to-day running of the team.	1 2 3 4
10	I communicate the vision to all team members.	1 2 3 4
11	I create opportunities for the team to work together and develop trust.	1 2 3 4
12	I encourage members to take on leadership roles in the team.	1 2 3 4
13	I provide clear feedback to all team members.	1 2 3 4
14	I focus on helping team members work together.	1 2 3 4
15	I encourage the team to review the way they work.	1 2 3 4
16	I encourage the team to coach and support each other.	1 2 3 4

Transfer your scores for each question onto the score sheet below, then add up each column to obtain the total score.

Q	A	Q	B	Q	C	Q	D
1		2		3		4	
5		6		7		8	
9		10		11		12	
13		14		15		16	
Total							

Your A score refers to the 'Director' style.
Your B score to the 'Orchestrator' style.
Your C score to the 'Facilitator' style.
Your D score to the 'Improvisor' style.

The questionnaire is based on the Leadership style and complexity model (shown in Figure 8.1) which explores how your style needs to change according to the experience and maturity of the team and the level of complexity it is operating in. It also recognises that you may need to adapt your approach to meet the challenges of day-to-day issues and events.

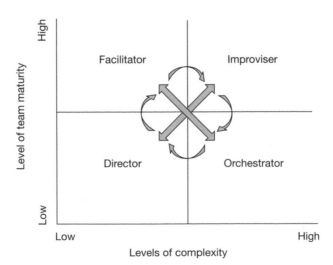

Figure 8.1 Leadership style and complexity

The Director style is one which literally gives strong direction. It is an assertive style which provides clarity on exactly what needs to happen by when. As a leader you will be leading from the front and will have formulated a clear vision and plan for what must be done. Your approach will be very hands-on, knowing what is happening in the team and providing strong steering and clear feedback in terms of how the work is progressing.

When to use this style:

- Project start-up when you may need to be clear about goals, direction and outcomes
- Working with inexperienced people who may not know what to do
- A crisis situation which requires clear instructions
- Working in situations when there is one clear answer and you are sure of the way forward

> ### Case study
>
> *Raj manages a team of site engineers. They work on projects around the region, and as skilled professionals have technical training to work independently and make decisions. However, whilst Raj recognises their expertise, he also needs them to deliver results for the division. There are cost constraints and time pressures on project completion. The division also has very high quality standards. As a result Raj is very directive about what he calls the 'must-do issues', the key deliverables he needs from the team. He provides clear outcomes with timescales so that the team are very aware of what they need to deliver and the parameters in which they have to work.*

As you can see, this style is valuable for setting up the team and defining the outcomes and expectations. However, if it is overused (for example if Raj was equally as directive about how the team worked on site) they would be unlikely to take responsibility and demonstrate initiative.

Behaviour breeds behaviour and if you continually use a directive style the team will let you make all the decisions and will be less enthusiastic about introducing new approaches and ideas. This in turn will have an enormous impact on your own time management as you literally try to be everything to everyone.

Complex situations, where you will certainly not know all the answers and where you need team members to act independently, will require you to think about other approaches. This is especially so if your team is working on topics where they are more technically expert than yourself, or they are working in a more dispersed team format where it is impossible for you to control everything.

If this is your predominant style your challenge will be one of learning to let go, to use this approach when needed but to balance it with the other three styles.

The Orchestrator role is one which focuses on providing the infrastructure and processes to succeed. You will be recognising and working with the talents of the team, providing coaching and creating the most efficient and effective working environment. The processes you set up could cover a whole range of activities such as establishing communication channels, review points, coaching, meetings, performance reviews, measurement and monitoring systems, all of which will help in the smooth running of the team.

Just like the conductor of an orchestra or band, you will know what you want to achieve, and will be conducting the team to accomplish your goal.

When to use this style:

- When you need to help the team form the infrastructure in which to work.
- When your team is dispersed and needs support to develop the communication processes and procedures to work together effectively.
- When team members are clear about their goals and outcomes but are not sure how to work together to achieve them.

- When team members have some experience and you can coach them to give of their best.
- When you are in a position to set up processes and ways of working which can help the team to achieve their work.

> ### Case study
>
> Ashley has responsibility for an IT support team spread across five different company sites. The team works on a shift basis to ensure continual support for staff. He established a number of processes to help the team operate efficiently. Monthly face-to-face meetings and weekly telephone conferences helped to iron out issues and focus on the introduction of new technologies. He also set up a measurement system to monitor the workload and customer satisfaction, and identify any recurring problems. Quarterly performance reviews were established and combined with coaching to help the team leaders work to their potential.
>
> The advantage of establishing clear processes meant that Ashley and his team knew how they were progressing. The regular contact enabled them to share issues and problems and gradually, as his confidence in the team grew, he was able to move into a more facilitative style.

The Facilitator style is far less directive than the previous two approaches described. As a leader you will be providing coaching and mentoring support. You will be helping the team by asking questions and assisting them in solving problems rather than providing the answers yourself. Your role will be far less hands-on and more concerned with helping the team to develop and grow. As the team has more experience you can use their knowledge and encourage them to take initiatives.

When to use this style:

- When neither you nor the team have all the answers and need to develop some new approaches.

- When you have the skills to facilitate and coach the team.
- When the team has the skills and ability to work effectively together.
- When you and the team have developed sufficient levels of trust in order to work together to create an environment of support and challenge.
- When you want to provide the space for the team to use their initiative and creativity and develop new ways of solving problems.

Case study

Simon works with a team of medical researchers. He recognises their skills and professionalism and whilst Simon has a research background he doesn't have the detailed knowledge his team have. In moving the project ahead he listens to the ideas from the team, posing questions, summarising what has been said and helping the group to come up with solutions to the issues they are currently facing. Given that the team are well aware of the deliverables and time constraints he uses this approach to keep the work on track and bring out the best in them.

Using this approach allows the team to find more creative solutions and also develop a greater sense of ownership in what they are doing.

The Improviser style is one where leadership is shared around the team. The vision will be created with the team and there will be recognition that all members have an important role in delivering success. Team members will be taking on responsibility for coaching and developing their colleagues and creating new ways of approaching their work. Ideas will be shared and you will be happy for the team to manage upwards, influencing the way you work and operate both within the team and with the external stakeholders. You will be comfortable letting go and trust that the team can deliver the results.

When to use this style:

■ When your team members are experienced and ready to take on responsibility.
■ When team members are willing and able to take on the role of coaching and developing others in the group.
■ When you are working on complex issues which require the creativity and expertise of the whole team.
■ When you are operating at a distance or don't have the time to be involved in everything.

Case study

Lyn headed up an internal PR team in a large organisation. She was constantly in meetings and spending time with other departments looking at how to improve the overall communication. Fortunately her team was experienced and worked well together. As a result they were able to take on much of the day-to-day activity. They coached and supported each other, set up sub-team meetings when necessary to focus on coming up with creative ideas, took decisions and ensured that projects were completed to a high standard. Lyn was regularly updated on what was happening and found that frequently she sought the ideas of the group to help move things forward. She trusted their expertise and valued the fact that they often came up with new and better ideas and took responsibility for implementing them.

The improviser role is often a scary one for team leaders to take on as it challenges all sorts of commonly-held assumptions about the leader as an heroic role model, leading from the front and having all the answers. However, it does mean that your team can be working to its potential and you can be free to support them from a more strategic angle to achieve their goal.

Facilitator	Improviser
• *Ad hoc* support when necessary. • Facilitating reviews, learning and performance management. • Coaching and mentoring role. • Unlikely to be involved in day-to-day running of the team • Creating opportunities for the team to develop and build trust.	• Shared leadership with the team. • Leader acts as coach and mentor along with team members. • The team uses initaitive and creativity to achieve goals. • Vision created together. • High level of trust developed. • Interdependence develops.
Director	**Orchestrator**
• Managing day-to-day workings of the team. • Establishing basic initial processes and ways of working. • Providing hands-on support to team members. • Delegating, monitoring and reviewing work.	• Setting up systems. • Accountable for setting vision, direction, common sense of purpose. • Agreeing ground rules, ways of working tailored to environment. • Establishing what's important. • Agreeing communication and governance processes. • Building skills and capabilites in the team.

Figure 8.2   Characteristics of the four leadership styles

Recognising the Need to Change

Developing flexibility is becoming more and more important. As we continue to work in complex environments, on problems which have no definable answer, and with a diversity of team members who may be specialists in their own areas, the need to flex and adapt as a leader is crucial. Using just one or two styles is not enough. Effective leadership requires the use of all the styles and the ability to recognise which approach will suit both the team and the context in which you are operating.

In reflecting on your approach you also need to think about how you want your team to be in the future. If you want your team to develop the maturity to take on more of a shared leadership style, you will need to focus on using the tools in Chapter 5 to help them to develop into a more highly performing team. As you are doing this you will also need to develop your behaviour so that the team starts to take initiative and develop their confidence. Only then will you and the team be able to operate in the improviser role.

It is therefore important to remember that team leadership is not something **you** do. It is something that **you and the team** need to do together in order to achieve success.

Leading Upwards and Outwards

Leadership not only involves leading your team, but also leading upwards and outwards. Managing your boss and other key stakeholders both inside and outside the organisation is part of your role as a strategic leader. It means that you will be in a better position to influence others, manage resources, deliver results and protect and promote your team.

Managing your Boss

During your career you will have upwards of 20 bosses, so understanding and working effectively with them is essential. The first step towards this is to put yourself into 'your boss's shoes' and reflect on the following questions:

- What issues/pressures are they facing?
- What are their targets and objectives?
- What is their working style?
- How do they react to stress?
- How busy are they right now?
- What are their strengths and weaknesses?
- How do they like to communicate?
- What do they want from you?

This will give you some insight into their issues, highlighting some of the misunderstandings that might be affecting your relationship. For example, simple things like the way you both communicate with each other can cause friction. You may have a more extrovert, 'talk it out' style, whilst your boss may prefer to be communicated with by email.

Once you have thought about your boss's approach and needs, reflect on your own style and how it differs from your boss.

- What is your work preference?
- What elements of your style would your boss approve of?

- What elements of your style would your boss find frustrating?
- What do you want from your boss in order to work effectively?

It's also useful to reflect on your own approach to authority. Are you someone who generally defers to authority, waiting to be told what to do, or are you a bit of rebel who likes to go off on their own, regarding any management as interference? What are the implications of this? Whatever your approach, you may need to think about adapting and finding a middle ground so that you and your boss can work together in an environment of mutual respect.

Managing your boss is like any other influencing situation. It's worth remembering that you are in a position to change the relationship, regardless of the power dynamics, just by what you do.

The list below outlines a number of things you can put into practice to develop and enhance your relationship.

1. **Take the opportunity to get to know each other.** Spending some quality time with your boss is important, so take the opportunity to work on an issue together, travel together, or spend some social time developing the relationship. Understanding more about your boss and their challenges can help you define more positive ways of working together.
2. **Have a conversation to define expectations.** This needs to be two-way, but you both need to discuss the expectations of the role and how you should to work together. This may change over time. For example, in the earlier stages of working together you may need to work more closely to ensure that you both have a common understanding of the issues and deliverables. However, as the relationship develops so too may the expectations change. You may feel ready to take on more responsibility and require less guidance.
3. **Adapt your communication style.** Find out their communication preference. Do they prefer text, emails, meetings or quick corridor chats? How much information do they like, detailed reports or one-page highlights? When do they want communication, on a weekly basis or just when you have something significant to report?
4. **Make sure you present solutions, not problems.** By all means have the occasional moan, but generally bosses like some alternative options

and ideas on how to implement them, so take time to think issues through, prepare a cost-benefit analysis and consider the consequences of different courses of action.

5. **Be consistent and reliable.** One important message is to be consistent and reliable in whatever you do. No boss wants to go round picking up the pieces along the way. Building up trust is an important part of managing your boss and the best way to do this is to deliver what you promise.

Managing your Network

Teams very rarely operate in isolation and there are usually a number of stakeholders who can influence the success and survival of a group. A stakeholder is literally anyone who has a stake in what you and the team are trying to achieve. They may be a project sponsor, a supporter or an ally. They may stand to benefit from what your team is doing or they may feel threatened. They may be working directly with the team or at a more senior level and in a position to influence the progress and success of what you are trying to achieve. They could also be either internal or external to the organisation.

Whoever they are, your challenge is to maximise the positive impact and minimise the negative impact they can have. One way of doing this is to map your stakeholders.

Take a piece of paper and in the centre draw your team. Add lines to represent all the different stakeholders you have. You can design the map to suit your specific needs and create your own ways of representing the different stakeholders by, for example:

- Using different colours to identify different locations, departments, etc.
- Identifying the level of the different sponsors by the length of the line from the centre with the longest line being the most senior.
- Using the thickness of the line for the quality of the relationship – a thick line representing a close relationship and a thinner or dotted line for a more distant relationship. You could use a jagged line to indicate if the relationship is a negative, problematic one.

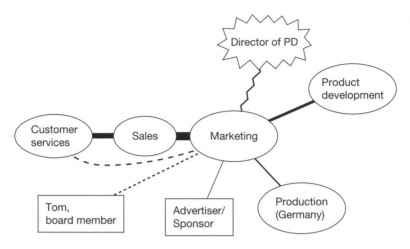

Figure 8.3 An example of a stakeholder map

Figure 8.3 is an example of a stakeholder map.

Once you have drawn your map, you can start to analyse it and reflect on the following questions.

- Do you have all the key stakeholders on the map, or should you include others?
- Do all the stakeholders have clear expectations about the purpose and deliverables of your team?
- Identify the stakeholders who support what the team is doing (indicate with a tick).
- Identify the stakeholders who could jeopardise what the team is trying to achieve (indicate with a cross).
- How can your supporters help you to achieve your goals?
- How can you minimise the effect of those who do not support your team?
- Who needs to be clear about the team's goals and deliverables?
- Who could help you gain extra resources?
- Who do you need to keep informed about what the team is achieving?
- Are you communicating well with all your stakeholders? What could you do to improve communication?

Once you have reached this stage you can start to think strategically about how to help your team by looking at:

- How to strengthen your network in order to support the work the team is doing.
- How to minimise the negative impact from stakeholders who do not support your team.
- How to ensure that you have sufficient positive support at senior management levels.

Case study

Carl was a global key account manager. He had a team of sales support people located around the world servicing a number of major clients. None of his team reported directly into him but part of their role was to provide product support and generate new accounts in their region. Carl was well aware that an important part of his leadership role was managing upwards and outwards. He needed to gain the support of the country managers so that they were happy for their people to be working this way. He also needed the support of the line managers of his team members and in addition he needed to ensure that he had senior level sponsorship from the board so that he could achieve his results. Without considering how to work with and influence each and every one of his stakeholders, Carl would have had difficulty in ensuring that the team had the time and resources to deliver for him.

Successful Influencing

Influencing is an essential skill not only in managing your stakeholders but also your team. Working in environments where you may not have direct power or authority but are expected to deliver results means that this skill is even more important in gaining the support you need.

In order to be an effective influencer you need to plan and develop your influencing strategy in order to ensure that you have the best possible chance of achieving your goal.

Figure 8.4 provides a strategy for developing and planning for any influencing situation.

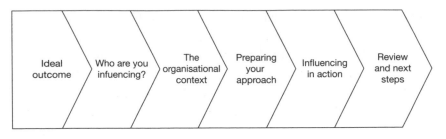

Figure 8.4 Developing your influencing approach

1. Identify your ideal outcome. This means being clear about what you will and won't be prepared to compromise on. Ideally in influencing, you want to go for a win-win situation. Think about how you can match the needs of others with your own.
2. Spend some time thinking about who you are trying to influence. What are their needs? These may be macro needs such as resources, deadlines and deliverables. There may also be more individual needs such as recognition, support, visibility and understanding. Use your questioning and listening skills to uncover the issues from their point of view.
3. Identifying the organisational context is also important. Who else is involved? Who are the stakeholders? What are the wider issues which may need to be considered? What style and approach works best in your organisation? Is there anyone who can help to influence on your behalf? All theses questions are encouraging you to explore the political dimension in which you work, illustrating that influencing involves thinking about the wider implications of what you are trying to achieve.
4. Having completed the first three stages of the strategy, you are now in a position to think about how you want to conduct the influencing conversation. You will need to think about the venue and the environment you want to create. You will also need to think about how you create rapport and what style and approach you want to adopt. Perhaps, even how you want to present yourself. Remember the more time spent planning, the more chance of success you will have.
5. Once you have completed your preparation you are in a good position to influence.
    - Start off by building rapport, creating common ground and trying to find a shared objective.

■ Take a flexible approach, remember to listen and ask questions and link in to their needs and concerns.

■ Remember to match the style of the other person and if you are persuading and making recommendations, remember to select three clear reasons to back up your ideas. Any more and you will face the possibility of diluting your argument and weakening your position.

■ Try to reach a joint agreement and use summarising to decide on the next steps and actions.

6. Finally, review the meeting. What went well and what could you do to improve? Remember, influencing is not a one-shot event and often it takes time and patience. You may need to reassess the situation, develop a new strategy and gain extra support from others to help to move towards your goal.

Summary

Team leadership is an important part of delivering performance through others. In order to be successful it is important remember to:

■ Develop flexibility in your leadership style so that you can use a range of approaches from Director, Orchestrator, Facilitator and Improviser.

■ Recognise that your style needs to change according to the levels of complexity you are working with and the maturity of your team.

■ Team leadership requires you to lead upwards and outwards in order to manage your boss and work with other key stakeholders who can influence the effectiveness and performance of your team.

■ Influencing effectively is a key component of team leadership and requires you to plan a clear influencing strategy to achieve your goal.

Conclusion

Reflecting on Your Learning Approach

The way you have used this book will have reflected the way you learn best. You will remember the concept of learning styles covered in Chapter 7.

As an **activist** you will have picked up on an idea in the book and immediately started to experiment with your team, testing whether it works for you by putting it into practice.

As a **reflector** you will have read a section and spent time thinking and reflecting on what it means and the consequences for yourself and the people you work with.

As a **theorist** the contents of this book will have raised questions for you about how you can explore the ideas in more depth. You will be intrigued to follow up on concepts and to explore the thinking behind the models.

As a **pragmatist** you will be focusing on the issues you are facing and using the book as a reference to find solutions to the problems you face.

Whilst it is always easier to work within your preference, this handbook provides you with the opportunity to move out of your comfort zone and try a different approach. As an activist it may be well worth quietly sitting back and thinking about the ideas in each chapter and how best to use them before you leap into action. On the other hand, if your approach is more of a reflector or theorist, encourage yourself to get in and have a go. Try some of the techniques with your team and you might be surprised by the results.

If you are curious to explore issues in more depth, follow up on theories and research, or find out more about the various questionnaires and tools which you could use with your team, use the information below to point you in the right direction.

Reading, References and Resources

Part 1 – Bringing out the Best in Others

Chapter 1 Motivating for Success

Reading and references

Breen, Bill (March, 2005), 'Clear Leaders', *Fast Company*.

Buckingham, Marcus and Clifton, Douglas (2002), *Now Discover Your Strengths: how to develop your talents and those of the people you manage*, Simon and Schuster.

Buckingham, Marcus and Coffman, Curt (2005), *First, Break All the Rules*, Simon and Schuster.

Chandler, Steve and Richardson, Scott (2004), *100 Ways to Motivate Others: how great leaders can produce insane results without driving people crazy*, Career Press.

Garvey, Charlotte (August, 2004), 'Meaningful Tokens of Appreciation', *HR Magazine*.

Kouzes, James and Posner, Barry (2003), *Encouraging the Heart: a leader's guide to rewarding and recognising others*, Jossey Bass.

McGregor, Douglas (2006), *The Human Side of the Enterprise*, McGraw-Hill.

Wallace, Julie (2001), 'After X Comes Y – echo boom generation enters workforce', *HR Magazine*.

Useful questionnaires and websites

1. The works interest schedule is a great questionnaire for tapping into the motivation profile of yourself and others. For more information contact http://www.mtsmanagement.co.uk
2. The strength deployment inventory is another useful instrument for exploring individual values and the impact on motivation: http://www.personalstrengths.co.uk
3. Shein, Edgar (1990), *Career Anchors: discovering your real values instrument*, Jossey Bass/Pfeiffer.

Chapter 2 Managing Performance Difficulties

Reading and references

Baron, Angela and Armstrong, Michael (2004), *Managing Performance*, Chartered Institute of Personnel and Development.

Fitts Hawley, Casey (2004), *201 Ways to Turn Any Employee into a Star Performer*, McGraw-Hill.

Jones, Pam (1999), *The Performance Management Pocketbook*, Management Pocketbooks.

Lombardo, Michael and Eichinger, Robert (1989), *Preventing Derailment: what to do before it's too late*, CCL Press.

Robertson, Alan and Abby, Graham (2003), *Managing Talented People*, Pearson.

Part 2 Building Effective Relationships

Chapter 3 Core Competences and Skills

Reading and references

Goleman, Daniel (1999), *Working with Emotional Intelligence*, Bloomsbury Publishing.

Kline, Nancy (1999), Time to Think: listening to ignite the human mind, Ward Lock.

Knight, Sue (2003), *NLP at Work*, Nicholas Brearley Publishing.

McDermott, Ian and O'Connor, Joseph (2003), *An Introduction to NLP*, Thorsons.

Useful questionnaires and websites

For more information on the emotional intelligence indicator (ECI) contact Hay Group http://haygroup.com

The Myers Briggs Type Inventory is a useful psychometric questionnaire to develop your self-awareness and understanding of others. For more information contact OPP Ltd http://www.opp.co.uk

Chapter 4 Essential Techniques

Reading and references

de Haan, Erik and Burger, Yvonne (2005), *Coaching with Colleagues*, Palgrave Macmillan.

Smart, J.K. (2003), *Real Delegation: how to get people to do things for you – and do them well*, Prentice Hall Business.

Starr, Julie (2003), *The Coaching Manual: The definitive guide to the process, principles and skills of personal coaching*, Prentice Hall Business.

Chapter 5 Practical Applications (or Productive Conversations)

Reading and references

Dale, Margaret (2003), *A Manager's Guide to Recruitment and Selection*, Kogan Page.

Eggert, Max (2003), *Perfect Counselling*, Arrow Books.

Fletcher, Clive (2004), *Appraisal and Feedback: making performance review work*, CIPD.

Part 3 Building High-Performing Teams

Chapter 6 Analysing Your Team

Reading and references

Canney-Davison, Sue and Ward, Karen (1999), *Leading International Teams*, McGraw-Hill.

Jones, Pam and Holton, Viki (2006), *Teams – Succeeding in Complexity*, Ashridge.

Katzenbach, Jon R. and Smith, Douglas J. (2001), *The Discipline of Teams: a mindbook-workbook for delivering small group performance*, John Wiley.

Willmore, Joe (2003), *Managing Virtual Teams*, Spiro Press.

Useful questionnaires and websites

For more information on Tuckman and his research into team development visit www.onepine.info

Chapter 7 Developing Your Team Tool Kit

Reading and references

Belbin, Meredith (2003), *Management Teams: why they succeed or fail*, Heinemann.

Coutu, Diane L. (May/June 1998), 'Trust in Virtual Teams', *Harvard Business Review*.

Fisher, Kimball and Fisher, Maureen (2001), *The Distance Manager*, McGraw-Hill.

Hofstede, Geert (2001), *Culture's Consequences*, Sage.

Katzenbach, Jon R. and Smith, Douglas J. (2005), *The Wisdom of Teams: creating the high-performance organization*, Harvard Business School Press.

Trompenaars, Fons (1993), *Riding the Waves of Culture*, Nicholas Brealey.

Useful questionnaires and websites

For more information on the Belbin team questionnaire go to www.belbin.com

For more information on the Thomas Kilmann conflict questionnaire contact OPP Ltd http://www.opp.co.uk/

For more information on learning styles contact www.peterhoney.com

Chapter 8 Team Leadership

Reading and references

Dent, Fiona Elsa and Brent, Mike (2006), *Influencing: techniques and skills for business success*, Palgrave Macmillan.

Forsyth, Patrick (2002), *Managing Upwards Pocketbook*, Management Pocketbooks.

Jones, P. and Holton, V. (2006), *Teams – Succeeding in Complexity*, Ashridge.

Williams, Colin, Wilke, Gerhard and Binney, George (2004), *Living Leadership*, Prentice Hall.

Index

READ ON ...

BRILLIANT MANAGER
What the best managers *know, do and say*
Nic Peeling
▶ £12.99 ▶ 0-273-70213-0 ▶ 978-0-273-70213-9

What the best managers *know, do and say*

Nic Peeling

Everything you've ever wanted to know about management – but were afraid to ask. This book is a refreshingly honest and practical guide to the best managerial practice, offering a handful of the most valuable things you need to know and do in a broad range of managerial situations. Read it, refer to it frequently and refresh your memory regularly. That way you'll be primed and prepared for every situation and will be on the managerial fast track for effectiveness and success.

You'll wonder how you ever managed without it...

FIVE STAR SERVICE ONE STAR BUDGET
How to create magic moments for your customers that get you noticed, remembered and referred
Michael Heppell
▶ £9.99 ▶ 0-273-70792-2 ▶ 978-0-273-70792-9

This book is the surest way to a more successful career for you and greater success for your organization. Bestselling author Michael Heppell shows you how the best customer service experience costs little if anything at all, but will win and retain you customers time after time, getting you noticed, remembered and referred. With over 100 instant tips, 50 examples of best practice, and multiple techniques and strategies, this book will equip you with a winning edge to impress your customers, deliver remarkable results, and fast track your career.

HOW TO LEAD
What you actually need to DO to manage, lead and succeed
Jo Owen
▶ £12.99 ▶ 0-273-69364-6 ▶ 978-0-273-69364-2

Whatever your level in an organisation, this indispensable and entertaining guide to the core skills of leadership is the practical handbook for getting to the top and staying there. With authoritative guidance and stimulating and entertaining advice, this guide tells you what you actually need to DO to manage, lead and ultimately succeed.

You can buy these books in all good bookshops,
or online at **www.pearson-books.com**

PEARSON
Prentice Hall
BUSINESS

THE RULES OF MANAGEMENT

A definitive code for managerial success

Is there a secret behind managerial success?

Yes – and this entertaining, informative and effective guide exposes the golden rules that should never be broken.

Offering practical advice, examples, hints and tips, this book reveals how you will make your managerial life smooth, effective and successful. Life will become easier, success greater, and although others will be good, you'll be even better.

Richard Templar
£10.99
0273695169
9780273695165

THE RULES SERIES

The Rules series is an international success and has sold over half a million copies worldwide.

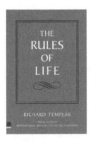

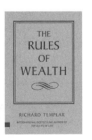

The Rules is a limited edition boxed set that brings together the bestselling The Rules of Life and The Rules of Work.

027370625X	0273662716	0273710192	1405846534
9780273706250	9780273662716	9780273710196	9781405846530

PEARSON
Prentice Hall
BUSINESS